JAMES JOHN GARTH WILKINSON: A MEMOIR OF HIS LIFE, WITH A SELECTION OF HIS LETTERS

Published @ 2017 Trieste Publishing Pty Ltd

ISBN 9780649617319

James John Garth Wilkinson: A Memoir of His Life, with a Selection of His Letters by Clement John Wilkinson

Edited by Trieste Publishing Pty Ltd.
Cover @ 2017

www.triestepublishing.com

CLEMENT JOHN WILKINSON

JAMES JOHN GARTH WILKINSON: A MEMOIR OF HIS LIFE, WITH A SELECTION OF HIS LETTERS

JAMES JOHN GARTH WILKINSON

J. J. Garth Wilkinson

JAMES JOHN GARTH WILKINSON;

A MEMOIR OF HIS LIFE, WITH A SELECTION FROM HIS LETTERS;

BY

CLEMENT JOHN WILKINSON.

"The things which are seen are temporal :
the things which are not seen are eternal."

LONDON
KEGAN PAUL, TRENCH, TRÜBNER & CO., LTD.
DRYDEN HOUSE, 43 GERRARD STREET, W.
1911

CONTENTS

CHAPTER I

CHAPTER II

CHAPTER III

CHAPTER IV

v

JAMES JOHN
GARTH WILKINSON

CHAPTER I

BIOGRAPHY

THE following fragment of autobiography was written
by Dr Wilkinson in 1872, but the task unfortunately
was abandoned or postponed.

James John Garth Wilkinson was born in Acton
Street, Gray's Inn Lane, London, on the 3rd of June
1812; the eldest of the family of James John
and Harriet Wilkinson; his father of Durham,
his mother of Sunderland.[1] His childhood was for
the most part spent in that neighbourhood, and he
played in the urban fields in which Acton Street
at that time ended.

[1] He was the eldest of eight children born to his parents. His
father came ultimately of Danish stock, and descended from a
professional family, whose arms (originally granted to one Lawrence
Wilkinson in 1615) still figure in the Town Hall of the City of
Durham. John James Wilkinson was a Special Pleader, and in
that capacity numbered at one time five Judges among his former
pupils; he was also for many years himself Judge of the Palatine
County Court in his native city, holding his jurisdiction from the
Prince Bishops of that day. Mrs Wilkinson, *née* Robinson, had
among her ancestors the Penn family, whence spring the founder
of Pennsylvania.

A

Notwithstanding the care of a tender mother, his childhood was full of dark shadows, partly from his own nature, partly arising from those around him. From his earliest recollection the thought of death pursued him ; chiefly the thought of the dead, which had been wrought into the fears excited by the horrible tales told him by the servants. These fears grew with his growth, and the anticipation of the darkness of night made the days wretched. This dread is the chief recollection of the days next to infancy. He was always afraid in his little walks of seeing some dead body carried in the streets. Opposite the window in Acton Street, in an enclosed field, there were fresh ox-skins hanging; these made a terrible impression for long. And once, in a journey to Sunderland by coach, among some nettles at the back of the hotel, he thinks at Grantham, he encountered a dead rat, and fell in fear among the nettles ; and was found, and brought to the coach. As time went on, the craving thought of the day was, how long the piece of candle allowed to go to sleep by should be. He generally outwatched the longest pieces, buried under the bedclothes. He was weak and ailing through his childhood.

From a dear religious mother he got no consolation ; nothing that took away superstitious terrors, or reconciled death with nature. His grandmother, Mrs Robinson of Sunderland, and his aunt, Mary Robinson, did their best to answer his questions, but the grave and its belongings were not to be disposed of. The horrors instilled into his mind by servants reigned supreme. Beyond the coffin and the vault no tale reached home to his heart.

The second woe of Acton Street was the parting from home in the morning to go to day-school in Gray's Inn Lane. It was an overwhelming sorrow, and lasted more or less all his schooldays. The contrast between grandmother and aunt and the rest of the world was unspeakably great and painful. And his shame was excessive at the red eyes which he took to school. The fear of the red eyes was the chief handle that could be used to quiet him.

These are the main points remembered: early affections tender, and reared in a hothouse to boot; and ghastly and ghostly fears from within and from without. One other recollection.

As a child he had a fatal facility of picking up bad words from the boys in the street, without in the least taking their meaning; and the occasional repetition of these at home entailed upon him severe punishment, sometimes exclusion from the family for several days. He remembers the bitterness of his mother coming into the little front parlour where he was confined with the servant, and not speaking to him, or allowing him to speak, because he had been wicked with his tongue. The remembrance, which may be a mistake, is as of a long period of durance.

He must have had pleasures during this period of his life ; but he does not recall them. For the rest, the circumstances remembered were poor enough, and the home comforts, and the home sweetness and cleanliness were far below what nurseries and children of the middle class at this day enjoy. Little eyes and noses are critical, and lay up as memories the smells and sights that are not proper, and protest against them inwardly, even though they have had no other experience to go by.

During these years he was taken to Sunderland by his aunt and grandmother, and well remembers the start in the coach from the great inn-yard, name forgotten (Saracen's Head ?), near Holborn Hill. There were boys going to a Yorkshire school as inside passengers, and when they had cried themselves to sleep, they slid down to the bottom of the coach. At Islington, passing the sheep pens there, he looked out, and asked if it was Sunderland. The journey for two or three days and nights continuously was a new world, and he remembers hill and dale, kind gentlemen on the way, the Yorkshire mountains in the right hand distance, tender interest in the little Yorkshire schoolboys, and on the last morning, the low stone walls on entering Sunderland, and then great aunt Maria Blakiston running by the coach-side for some distance before the coach reached its destination.

He does not know if this was his only early visit

to Sunderland ; but if it was he might be seven years old, and he spent a year with his aunt and grandmother in the North.

But he is probably anticipating. Before the year in Sunderland the family removed from Acton Street to a better house in the New Road, No. 8 Seymour Place, opposite to where New St Pancras Church now stands, but which at that time was a region of nursery gardens, extending nearly from Battle Bridge (now King's Cross) to Tottenham Court Road. Here he remembers some of the births of his brothers and sisters. He now went to school to the Misses Norgate in Burton Street, and for the first time, as it appears, had other children for friends and companions. He calls to mind no learning, but friendly schoolroom battles, side against side, in which the little combatants rushed shouting at each other, and the shock was glorious to relate at home. One incident fixed itself, and was not understood. A governess in Miss Norgate's school in a fit of anger cut off all her own hair.

Next he went to school to Miss Grover, living in a street off Euston Square, whose father was Master of the St Pancras National Schools. Sometimes his father took him and his brother William on Sunday after church to the National School, and placed them in class there, and he felt surprise and sense of power in the multitude of boys assembled. At Miss Grover's for the first time he began to learn,

and to like learning ; and at the end of one half year
he received for prize a silver pencil case which then,
as now, was like no other silver pencil case. It
can be recollected without an effort, which is not
the case with others. Miss Grover was a neat,
trim, kind young lady, both precise and persuasive,
and he well remembers the sweetness of her influence ;
he saw her the day before her death a year or two
ago, still fine, trim and sweet, unspoilt by her passage
through the world, and little changed by her clean
old age.

All this time the ghastly fears went on, and dreams,
nothing in themselves, influenced the years. One
dream was full of mortality. It was a dream of a
procession of swans, a funeral procession, as it were,
walking funereal plumes, coming down the New Road,
and entering a great vaulted cathedral with tombs
around. The spirit of death was strong in the dream.
Another experience of sleep was not a dream but a
sensation as of infinity in the substance of the
brain ; a feeling of the sands of infinity ; from
what he now knows a kind of anatomical feeling
of the pulp of the brain itself acted upon by some
subtle overwhelming influence, which gave no pain,
but was soft, smooth, and horrible to bear and to
remember. It occurred now and then, and he
generally woke with it, for if it had lasted it seemed
as if it must destroy him. In his waking hours
about this time, once for several days, he had the

impression of having committed the sin against the Holy Ghost, and the misery of being inconsolable by his dear mother, aunt, and grandmother, of being beyond their kind boundaries in his thought, was bewildering. This state soon passed away under their kind ministrations.

Another strange thing was that being for his age a good penman—the pencil case, he thinks, was for penmanship—he wrote on ruled lines in a little book prayers to the Devil, full of bad words; he felt powerfully moved to write them, and a sense of independence in the act. These peculiarities are nearly all that stands out at this time. The fatal swans, the smooth horror rolling in his head during sleep, the despair of unpardonable sin, and the doing what he liked in the prayers to the wicked one. Straws of influences and nothing more, but they seemed then as now to belong to the life of life.

Probably he was taken from Miss Grover's excellent eye, to make the journey to Sunderland already mentioned. The year passed in the North was the first year of remembered pleasures; the aunt and grandmother were at Sunderland, and he was their boy. He was there placed at school, and being an exceedingly timid and shamefaced boy, he held his own with great difficulty among other boys; they perceived his want of resistance, and invaded it, as boys do by their law of pressure, without mercy. He recollects learning nothing but the multiplication table ; with one horrible exception, dancing. Having no ear for music, and unbounded shame about his own person, utter absence of ease or pleasure even in the movement of walking before others, dancing was a degradation unspeakable. It revolted him. The fear of being let into it made it impossible to get him to children's parties, where it might occur, and where also games of forfeits in which some penalty of action, such as kneeling in the middle of a room, might be demanded of him. His greatest trial in Sunderland was the ball of the dancing school at the Assembly Rooms, round which were ranged parents and friends in appalling numbers. He had to take part in one dance, and his face, and body, and arms, and legs were all made of shame ; he just lived through it. No one knew what it cost, or how little his degrada- tion of nature could be consoled or reached from without. The deepest depth of it all was that in the whole matter he was in partnership, forced partner- ship, with little girls, who were beings he could not understand ; he was so ashamed of them and of himself. He is not quite sure that the " soft smooth horror " of his sleep was not the spirit of all these shames ; the gulf by which they got into his brains.

But he had also more boyish experiences in the North, and occasionally took part with the rough lads of whom the school consisted in raids and forays in the town. The sense of the power of gathered boys, their numbers, their mighty shouting, excited and delighted him. It was as a unit, when eyes seemed turned on him, that his weakness came.

At holiday times, and on half holidays, he used to go to Ryhope, to his grandmother's cottage there, where he was completely happy. The milk-boys on donkeys, seated between two barrels of milk, came in from Ryhope to Sunderland, and, whenever he was permitted, he rode back with Jemmy Bone, the son of his grandmother's tenant, between the empty barrels, and spent the night at dear Ryhope. The farmyard, the granary, the straw-loft, the little garden full of gooseberry bushes with a high stone wall round it, Ryhope pond, the largest inland water he had seen, a long strip of water deeply and mysteriously abutting on fenced fields, mysteriously because who could imagine the depth there, and with many swallows playing over it, all these were adequate blessings to his childhood. The road through a gate of whale jaw-bones along beautiful lanes to the Tunstall Hills, to a small property of his father's called Holichar Sides ; the walk to Ryhope Dean, the most romantic spot he had then seen, and the little village of Seaham ; and the path from the bottom of the village of Ryhope to the sea, are still his most precious memories of scenery.

The picnic of picnics happened to him in this year ; his father was at Sunderland, and a large party of ladies and gentlemen went along the coast towards Castle Eden in a covered van ; a merry and uproarious party. At the destination he strayed away among the fells, and there found mountain bushes, junipers, and other plants of such regions, which were as parts of a new world to him. And on the same day in a rocky cove he came upon a moored boat, and got into it, when it went out to sea to the length of its rope, and the situation, with its beauty of clear depth of water, seemed and always will seem the beginning of adventure. The number of new things in the world this day, and the largeness of them, surprised him. He found to his inexpressible satisfaction that there were such places as wilds. It was like being let into a large property which made the former poverty apparent.

This day stands out. And also in this year another of the Bones, in the summer evenings, used to take his gun, and go out with the boy to shoot small birds in the hedges; " yellow yowlies " sometimes, and even blackbirds. His delight in a gun was very great; it was the most beautiful of objects, the possession of it betokening manhood. He was fond to a degree of having and admiring the dead birds; he loved them, and had no idea of wrong done them; and though he knew they were killed, he had never been told there was inhuman cruelty in the act, and so he loved to see them shot, and loved them afterwards. The passion for a gun went all through his boyhood, though he had none of the physical faculties which make a sportsman. It was the first romance of the power of skilful destruction ; the penetration with this into beautiful parts of nature ; and the possession of the coy birds unwilling to be acquired. There must have been a good many young passions in it or it could not have been so fascinating.

These small pieces of memory are nearly all that survives of this delightful year, in which he was surrounded by grandmother and aunts and great aunts, and at home as he had never been before. One dear old friend of the family, Miss Ridley, of Villiers Street, Sunderland, was equal to any of his relations in her kindness, and the jargonel pear-tree in her garden was a part of her sweetness. Old Molly and younger Betty, her servants, were among his best kindred, and they so conceited him that he used to deliver long and loud addresses caught from the scant politics of the parlour, from the kitchen dresser. He thinks they were either for or against Queen Caroline ; but that is doubtful. No stream of this public speaking has entered into his later life. He was evidently a very timid, shamefaced boy, with strong feelings and vivid words when they dared to come out; and very very ignorant of control except by timidity, and of the consequences to himself or others when he let his passions and actions go free.

His maternal great granny died when he was at Sunderland, and this fed his fear of death, which otherwise abated during this year, because grandmother or aunt were always near him, awake and asleep. He could not be got into the house where his good old ancestor's body lay.

At last a strange morning came at Ryhope, a morning known for some time to be coming. He was to go back to his parents in London. That morning he was indulged with loving indulgence, and granny and Aunt Mary were with him heart and soul to the last. He plucked a blue Iris bud—I see it now—from the little front garden of the cottage; and then the coach from Sunderland to London stopped at the gate; he was given into some old gentleman's charge, and he remembers nothing more but that he commended him for the journey, guarded his lily for him, and I suppose took him home to Seymour Place. He does not recall the meeting at home, in which he sank into one of several; his mother was ever dear and warm; but his aunt and granny had become his mother.

Shortly after this he met his brother, William Martin Wilkinson; he was staying in the country, I think at Perry Hill, and he was taken thither; the meeting was in a field. He had looked forward to it ignorantly but with desire; and when they had rushed into each other's arms, he was amazed that he could not speak, and was crying. It struck him as so odd that he was crying, and yet so happy to have his brother.

He might now be about nine years old, and there

were four or five sisters and brothers of them at home.

Here the fragment of autobiography comes to an end, before the middle of that period in each life which is particularly sparse of preserved details. It does not present a picture of happy childhood ; without indicating anything morbid in the child, it suggests self-analysis and introspection, though these qualities were in reality perhaps the thoughts of adult life unconsciously transferred back to the events and times which they concerned.

It must have been soon after his return from Sunderland that the boy was sent a large private school at Mill Hill, kept by Messrs Thorowgood and Wood, who moved, during his pupilage, to Totteridge in Hertfordshire. The few letters of this date which have been preserved are mainly interesting by reason of requests for books from home. The boy thanks his father for having sent him Milton's poems. " I am sorry to say that Mr Thorowgood opened the parcel and took " Roderick Random " away, because he did not think it proper for me to read." He asks at various times for Seele's " Analysis of the Greek Metres," Anacreon's odes, " The Lady of the Lake," " The Lay of the Last Minstrel," Campbell's " Theodoric " and " The Pleasures of Hope," also for Sir William Jones' poems. He is taking in Lord Byron's poems as they appeared in serial numbers, and speaks of spending some of the money which he

brought with him in books. In 1826 he gained a
prize for a poem of one hundred and sixty lines upon
" Babylon," and copies out all but sixteen lines,
" which were no great beauty to it," for his father.
This success justifies the requests for poets and gives
evidence of some early taste for versification, interesting in view of his later production of Improvisations
of the Spirit.   He appears to have had some dealings
with chemicals, as he was fined for burning his coat
with sulphuric acid.   He lost his mother in 1825.
His frequent and long visits to his grandmother and
aunts at Ryhope, had made him little of a " mother's
boy," but her early death practically ended Garth
Wilkinson's knowledge of home life until he made a
home for himself on his marriage.   He left Totteridge
with a very favourable report in 1829.   He maintained a friendship with Mr Thorowgood until the
death of that gentleman in 1860.   On parting with
his pupil, Mr Thorowgood said : " Now mind you,
you keep up your Latin, you'll want it," a prophetic
remark to one who was to spend much labour in
translating the Latin of Swedenborg.

The boy was now sixteen, and had probably made
as good progress in classics and English literature
as could be expected from one of his years.   The
time had come for him to choose a career.   " Now,
James, I want you to choose your profession," said
his father.   " I want to be a lawyer," the boy
answered.   " I don't think that would suit you,"

was the reply. " I have already made arrangements for you to be with Mr Leighton at Newcastle, to be a surgeon." The advice of parents was apt to be peremptory in 1829; but the medical profession specially demands self-devotion and aptitude ; and it cannot be regarded as anything but a dangerous experiment to throw a young and sensitive lad on to its avenues not only without, but even against, his expressed wishes.

Thomas Leighton was senior surgeon to the Infirmary of Newcastle-on-Tyne. The bond for the performance of covenants, etc., set forth in an Indenture of Apprenticeship, was signed by Mr Wilkinson, senior, on June 4, 1828, that being, as it happened, the day following Garth Wilkinson's sixteenth birthday.

His experience as a medical student, under apprenticeship and in hospital, was almost contemporary with those of Albert Smith's " Mr Ledbury " and Dickens' Bob Sawyer and Ben Allen. He has left no details of them; but it is plain that, as the pupil of a senior surgeon to one of the best of the provincial hospitals, he would act as his master's " dresser " and be brought into practical contact with such surgical work as was done in those pre-antiseptic and pre-anæsthetic days; his other duties consisted, no doubt, of drug-compounding and of bleeding, and otherwise treating those whom his master could delegate to a pupil. Whatever he

saw and did at this time, and for long afterwards,
had little effect in reconciling the child who suffered
daily and nightly terrors over the apparatus and
mystery of death to the practice of surgery or
medicine as boy or man.[1]   Wilkinson, as he himself
said, at a much later date, was " schooled to bear
a dresser's part in the wards and in the operations
known and practised in that day, but hated them.
He knows what surgery means.   From his very entry
into the shop of the Old Way, he never believed in
the good or truth of promiscuous drugging."   It
was not until many years afterwards, when he had
embraced Homœopathy, that he could say that
" he loves the healing art of which Homœopathy is
the present crown," or that he could write : [2]—

" What is best, I take a leading interest in my
dear Medicine, and especially in Homœopathy, and I
reckon myself truly fortunate to be able *at length*
to connect my mind to my daily work ; and to see
in the latter a most ample field for the exercise of
my thoughts."

But the routine education of an unwilling pupil
left him ever hostile to the *Profession* into which
it introduced him.   Swedenborg prepared him

---

[1] Some idea of the disgust which the hospital routine of the early
nineteenth century inspired in one who was destined to become a
surgeon of world-wide reputation, can be gathered from Syme's
Address on Surgery, delivered before the British Medical Association
in 1865.

[2] Letter to Mr Henry James, November 14, 1852.

for Homœopathy, and Homœopathy taught him to love the healing art; but in 1870, when he was a registered practitioner of thirty-six years' standing, he wrote his pamphlet "A Free State and Free Medicine," advocating, in his own words, universal discharterment of medical bodies, and an embracive penal code for illegitimate operations and deadly drugging: every mortal operation and fee, to be the subject of (? for) a jury.

In 1832 he came back to London, "walked" Guy's Hospital for two years, and qualified as Member of the Royal College of Surgeons and Licentiate of the Society of Apothecaries in June 1834. He was granted the degree of M.D., *honoris causa*, by the University of Philadelphia in 1853. Once qualified in his profession, the necessity for maintaining himself became pressing, and the young surgeon lost no time in setting to work. He found this first as a locum tenens at Aylesbury.

This engagement was necessarily a temporary one, and on November 9, 1835 we find Garth Wilkinson, helped by loans from his grandmother and his maternal uncle, William Sewell, at the Veterinary College, establishing himself as an independent medical practitioner at 13 Store Street, Bedford Square. The position of a medical man in private practice differed then from that which he at present enjoys; it was more that of an apothecary than of a physician. Though called

B

upon to diagnose the diseases of his patients, and charging for these services a small fee for attendance, the greater part of his profits lay in dispensing his own prescriptions and in selling drugs and plasters over the counter of his " front shop " : the " back-parlour " was often at once a consulting-room and living room. The system was an unsatisfactory one : for the patient, because it exposed him to the necessity of swallowing drenches and boluses in large numbers and quantity ; for the practitioner in general, because it concentrated his interest and attention upon routine prescribing and petty profit ; for Garth Wilkinson in particular, because he, as we know, " never believed in the good or truth of promiscuous drugging." But it was the custom of that day ; and a man without capital, influence, or academic distinction was in no position to upset or defy it.

But, while we have been following the education and outset of our young medico, some extra-professional events had occurred which were to exercise strong and lifelong influence upon the development of his character and the nature of his work. One of the brothers of his mother lived at Woodford in Essex, and he was a devout reader and follower of Emanuel Swedenborg. On a visit to this uncle, Mr George Robinson, Garth Wilkinson received his first introduction to the voluminous writings of the great Swedish mystic. Little as he or his introducer could guess it, the initiation was an event far reaching both for the man and the doctrines. For the neophyte it was the opening of conscious spiritual life, the first rapt sight of possibilities for himself and his fellows; possibilities to the development and promulgation of which he was himself to devote the longest hours and deepest thoughts of a long life of deep thinking and earnest humble work. For the doctrine it was light and expression. For two generations of time the writings had lain buried in a dead language, under an accumulation of neglect all but universal. The time was ready for their resuscitation, and the man who could effect their freedom appeared. If genius is the coincidence of the hour and the man, a Swedenborgian genius was then engendered. It was here, too, and almost at the same time, that Swedenborg's champion met the companion who was to comfort and encourage him along the path which was opening before them all unwitting. Miss Emma Anne Marsh, daughter of Mr William Marsh, of Diss, Norfolk, was governess to Mr Robinson's family. The meeting, late in 1833, was at once recognized as momentous by the young man, and two years later he was to learn that he shared the recognition with her. There was the inevitable pleasing torment of doubts and fears, but on December 12, 1835, an engagement was entered into and announced. It is not difficult

to think that the two events were complemental.
So at least thought one of the contracting parties.
Writing on the second anniversary of the engage-
ment, he says :—

" This gloomier end of the year is now memorable
to me for two remarkable circumstances of my
life; I mean my betrothing to thee, and my
acquaintance with the writings of Swedenborg; two
events which, occurring almost in the same month,
have something spiritually of connexion with each
other.   I can most truly say that I wish my reception
of both of you to be constantly progressing; I
don't feel in either case that my affections are
lessened; I do not find that a nearer inspection
dissipates the fair things I have admired in both;
and I do pray that we may be enabled to live over
the glorious things which are held out to us in those
books of which I hope we have something of a
common admiration."

From the time of his engagement to Miss Marsh,
letters passed between the *fiancés* at nominally
weekly intervals, though there were not seldom
occurrences which made even more frequent communication seem necessary. This long series of
letters (for they were not married until January
4, 1840) would make it possible to construct a
diary of Garth Wilkinson's doings, hopes and fears,
and of many of his thoughts and aspirations. The
fluctuations of practice, pecuniary anxiety, his social

pleasures, his early literary labours, his judgments of men and measures, are all set down in this *journal intime*; but what concerns us more is the evidence which it contains of growing character. The early letters are those of a young man, little more than a boy truly in love—

> Just for the obvious human bliss,
> To satisfy life's daily thirst
> With a thing men seldom miss.

But as the time goes by, responsibility and work, professional and literary, each piece done honestly, ponderings over the pages he translates, and over the Introductions which he writes, do their work. Some of the toil would have been sordid and souring to one less in earnest; but we see the writer of pretty and sincere love-letters developing into the strong loving man, just and firm of purpose, tender to his fellows but hateful of the evil which comes between them and their Maker: self reliant but humble. It is a process which does not lend itself to illustration by quoted passages, but the change is writ plain in the letters and could scarcely fail to be discerned.

It is not clear whether the purchase of the lease of 13 Store Street carried with it the goodwill of a medical predecessor, or whether the venture was a breaking of new ground. In either case, the amount of work to be found was small, at first very small;

and there was ample time for other occupations
not incompatible with waiting for patients.
Wilkinson's mind was now fully engaged in the
study of Swedenborg's writings, and he was already
in touch with the Swedenborgian Society. He
began a course of reading in his many spare hours,
and gives an account of himself at the British Museum
Reading Room of that day.[1]

" Fancy to yourself three very large and splendid
rooms, equalling the King's library in the whole
length of the suite, and filled with all the thinking,
literary, and antiquarian faces in London, with deep
silence prevailing over the whole assembly, and you
will have a picture of a curious kind. 'Tis like a
huge schoolroom, where all the (old) boys are really
bent on improvement, each man having before him
some huge old tome, and in general a notebook, into
which he is transcribing the cream of wisdom." He
appears impressed by the example of his seniors, to
have opened his studies in a " History of Philosophers,"
and marked that all were mentioned but Swedenborg.

His zeal for the cause, and his evident desire to
spend his energies in furthering it, soon led to his
obtaining a commission from the Swedenborgian
Society for a translation from the Latin of their
master. It was a huge piece of work : the translator
passed through the usual stages of hope, despair, of
plodding and feverish work. These moods are reflected

---

[1] Letter to Miss E. A. Marsh, August 8, 1836.

in his correspondence. At one time he writes, " I am now quite certain that authorship is not my *forte*: nay, that it is not possible to me "; at another, " I have been steadily and methodically getting on with the Translation of the ' Doctrine of Charity,' the corrected copy of which I have now half finished. I think I improve in translating ; and especially in gradually gaining a finer perception of the *minutiæ* of meaning in the author's Latin ; for there are many things which a person might never know, without being detected in any grievous omission, but which, if he does know, will gradually give a finished accuracy and an air of refined meaning, which the reader will feel, if he does not intellectually detect it. Such are the renderings of many little words, and many short arms of sentences, which frequently occur, and which have always been stumbling-blocks. I think I am now getting a few formulas in my head for some of them, and when I have done this I can readily and rapidly apply my knowledge."

He worked, through good cheer and evil cheer, to such purpose that, having already published his translation of the " Last Judgment " and " Fall of Babylon," in November 1839 he is correcting at the same time proofs of a volume of his own translation of the " Arcana Cœlestia " and of a volume of the " Doctrine of Charity " in Swedenborg's original Latin. Even before the latter was published, he was contemplating a new and amended edition of it ; and had also laid out for himself another heavy piece of work.

" [1] I have set myself another task ; and, not without invoking the Divine Blessing. I have actually commenced it ; and am determined to ' do or die.' This task is, the translation into English of Swedenborg's great work entitled ' Regnum Animale ' or Animal Kingdom ! It contains seven hundred closely printed quarto pages, and I shall be about three years in completing it ; but when I have, I trust, if I work with a good *end* (the end is *all*), I shall have shown that God intended a use to His children even through me, and in manifestly becoming such an instrument, and in most humbly becoming so, lies the only, the greatest, glory which can belong to anyone, to woman or to man. I calculate upon doing a page a day, and I hope you will sit beside me and encourage me to my duty. I do not intend to be in a hurry about it, nor yet in an apathy. . . . The advantages will be great (as to money, probably, in the first instance, *none*). They will be, first, disconnected from self, the boon to the English Public, and especially the Medical Profession, of the greatest and noblest work on Human Physiology which has ever appeared in the world ; and the disposing men's minds thereby to look upward to the still more glorious truths which the author of the work was the instrument of dispensing. Nothing can be better calculated to effect this, than

[1] Letter to Miss Marsh, October 8, 1839.

the ' animal kingdom.' It has solidity and depth, beauty, philosophy, Reverence and Fact! and all these things in the highest degree. The advantages to me will be, that the translating of the work will lead me through the whole field of Physiology (the most important one in medicine) as disclosed in this and in many other authors; and this will make me a far more able professor of medicine. It will give me a perfect facility in reading and knowing the Latin language, and even some power of writing it, if need be. It will make me a fair English writer, and accustom me to the model of the finest writer of any age or country. And it will give me a certain standing among the men of letters in the land, if I do it well. Then, the greatest and first and last of reasons, I shall be fulfilling a use for which, since He gave me the power, I may think that the Lord designed me. I am going on, therefore, and go on I will."

The work was begun in a high spirit; it was one which it needed high spirit to attack. It was longer and harder than he who undertook it knew; but he finished it, and it was duly published in 1843.

But these were not to be the first fruits from Garth Wilkinson's pen to reach the public eye.

In 1838, Mr Charles Augustus Tulk, then Member of Parliament for Poole, lent Mr Wilkinson a copy of William Blake's "Songs of Innocence and of Experience," a copy of William Blake's own making. The "Songs," issued in many a modern series of

English classics, are now to be found on many book-shelves, and in many memories; but in 1838 they existed only in the prints struck off from the copper upon which Blake had himself engraved in relief both the text and the marginal illustrations. Of the thirty pence which Blake and his wife owned for their sole resource, on one occasion, twenty-two were spent in the purchase of materials for the first impressions. Surely determination to be heard could no further go. The delicacy and spiritual simplicity of the "Songs" made a deep impression on Garth Wilkinson, who was himself to do somewhat similar work in his Improvisations from the Spirit. His brother William, holding no lower opinion, came forward with the necessary funds; subscribers were sought high and low; a preface was written, and the edition (the first *printed*, in the usual sense of the word), a thin cloth-bound octavo, was published jointly by Pickering and Newbery on July 9, 1839. It consists of twenty-one pages of preface and seventy-four pages of text. It is a little book, which now finds a big welcome from bibliophiles. Mr Gilchrist had difficulty in obtaining it in 1860, when nearly thirty shillings was its usual price. At five times that sum it may be sought for in vain to-day; but its editor thought himself fortunate to introduce it to his generation without loss. In his preface, after de-tailing the then known facts of Blake's life, our young author sets himself to examine the spiritual claims of his poet. He falls foul of Allan Cunningham, who roughly classed them as delusions. He says, " In thus condemning the superficial canons by which Blake has been judged, it is far indeed from our intention to express any approbation of the spirit in which he conceived and executed his latest works ; or to profess to see good in the influences to which he then yielded himself, and from which his visional' experiences proceeded. But since every human being, even during his sojourn in the material world, is the union of a spirit and a body the spirit of each being among spirits in the spiritual, even as his body is among bodies in the natural world—it is therefore plain, that if the mind has unusual intuitions, which are not included by the common laws of nature and of body, and not palpable to the common eye, such intentions must be regarded as spiritual facts or phenomena ; and their source looked for, in the ever-present influences—Divinely provided, or permitted, according as they are for good or evil—of our own human predecessors, all now spiritual beings, who have gone before us into the land of life. On this ground, which involves the only pratical belief of the immortality of the soul, and the only possibility of the past influencing the present, it would be un-philosophical and even dangerous, to call our very dreams delusions. It is still, indeed, right that we ' try all spirits, at the judgment bar of a revelation-enlightened reason '; yet, be the verdict what it may,

it can never retrospectively deny that spiritual
existence, on whose qualities alone it is simply to
adjudicate."

This is, of course, a short statement of the
Swedenborgian teaching concerning the factors which
condition "influx," and it is supported by a foot-
note: "The true and unpopular doctrine on this
subject is so plainly set forth by our great modern
luminary, that we ask no excuse for inserting it here;
more especially as it will assist the reader to the comprehension of Blake's state of mind." There follows
a long Latin quotation from Swedenborg.

The preface goes on to appreciate Blake's artistic,
and especially his poetic, position. Speaking of
Blake's terrible drawings of hell, it says : " We have
the impression that we are looking down into the
hells of the ancient people, the Anakim, the Nephilim,
and the Rephaim. Their human forms are gigantic
petrifactions, from which the fires of lust, and intense
selfish passion, have long since dissipated what was
animal and vital; leaving stony limbs, and counten-
ances expressive of despair and stupid cruelty."
Blake's mind is then compared and contrasted with
that of Shelley. The preface concludes: "If the
volume gives one impulse to the New Spiritualism
which is now dawning on the world; if it leads one
reader to think that all reality for him, in the long
run, lies out of the limits of space and time; and that
spirits, and not bodies, and still less garments, are

men ; if it gives one blow, even the faintest, to those
term-shifting juggleries, which usurp the name of
' Philosophical Systems ' (and all the energies of all
the forms of genuine truth must henceforth be expended on these effects), it will have done its work
in its little day, and we shall be abundantly satisfied
with having undertaken to perpetuate it, for a few
years, by the present republication."

This preface appears to call for somewhat extensive quotation, primarily as being the first
original work of Wilkinson's pen ; and, secondarily,
as being difficult of approach for the general
reader. The vivid vigour of style and some of
the curious knowledge of the writer are already
visible.

The drawings of Blake deeply impressed his
admirer. " A few days ago," he writes on November
6, 1838, " I was introduced by my friend Mr Elwell
to a Mr Tathans, an artist, who possesses all the
drawings left by Blake. . . . It was indeed a—
not a treat, but an astonishment to me. The first
painting we came to realized to me the existence
of powers which I did not know are had in it. 'Twas
an infernal scene, and the only really infernal thing
I ever saw—' Life *dies*, Death lives ' might, as
Elwell said, explain the character of it. It was most
unutterable and abominable—a hopeless horror.
Of the same kind were many of the others. On the
whole, I must say the series of drawings, giving me

an idea that Blake was inferior to no one who ever
lived, in terrific tremendous power, also gave me
the impression that his whole inner man must have
been in a monstrous and deformed condition—
for it teemed with monstrous and horrid productions.
Those who would see Hell *before* they die, may be
quite satisfied that they veritably have seen it by
looking at the drawings of Blake. At the same
time, all the conceptions are gigantic and appropriate,
and there is an awful Egyptian death-life about all
the figures."

A belief in the truly spiritual nature of Blake's
inspiration is not inconsistent with deep suspicions
as to his sanity. " I received," he wrote on July
17, 1839, " the Designs, etc., of Blake's from Mr
Clarke; comprising, I fancy, all those you saw. I
almost wish I had not seen them. The designs
are disorder rendered palpable and powerful, and
give me strongly the impression of their being
the work of a madman. Insanity seems stamped
on every one of them; and their hideous forms
and lurid hellish colouring, exhale a very unpleasant
sphere into my mind; so much so, that I confess
I should not like to have the things long in my
house. . . . I felt puzzled what to say of the man
who was compounded of such heterogeneous materials
as to be able at one time to write the ' Songs of
Innocence ' and at another ' The Visions of the
Daughters of Albion.' ' The Book of Thel ' is, partly,

an exception to the general badness or unintelligibility of his verse and designs. I *can* see some glimmer of meaning in it, and some warmth of religion and of goodness; but beginning to be obscured and lost under the infatuating phantasies which at length possessed its author. I should say sanity predominates in it, rather than that the work was a sane one. Some of the single lines are grand and expressive."

But when a man is between twenty-five and thirty, and a bachelor (though quite unwillingly), and full of interest in life, physic and translation cannot occupy all his time. His friend Mr Dow lived in or near Store Street, and had a large and pleasant circle of acquaintance into which he cordially welcomed his young doctor. Mr Tulk, too, had reunions of varying degrees of formality, where at one time set debates on matters Swedenborgian took place; at others general social pleasures were pursued. Among his brother professional men he naturally made many friends, while as yet he had not banished himself from among them by championing the unpopular doctrines of Hahnemann. He made the acquaintance of Robert Browning, and heard a private reading of " Strafford " at Mr Dow's before seeing the first performance of the play on May 1, 1837. " You are curious to hear about ' Strafford.' Well, you shall be told. . . . We all formed a formidable body at the box door;

. . . there were three dozen of us together. The house was crammed to the utmost, and the audience very respectable. The first Act went off rather heavily, but the play gained as it proceeded, and in spite of a most miserable ' cast of characters,' it must be considered a most successful production. The applause at its termination was prodigious, and lasted for something like twenty minutes, mingled with the most vociferous cries for the author, who, however, did not appear."

" Last night (Feb. 3, 1838) Mr Browning, senior, came here. He is a very pleasant and quiet man, and Mr Dow made him sit down with pencil in hand and produce a little off-hand sketch of Baby. In three or four minutes he produced a very striking likeness."

He had some acquaintance with Macready, saw him in " Virginius " and found it " a perfect master-piece of acting, and far too much for my sensibilities." " You will be sorry to hear that on Friday night (April 1836) Mr Macready was greatly irritated by the conduct of Mr Bunn, the rascally manager of Drury Lane, and was tempted to give Mr Bunn a very complete and merited thrashing. . . . Mr Dow was there at the time." The " Poet " Bunn and the readily irritated tragedian must have made a fine scene.

About this time he attended lectures on Animal Magnetism by Baron Dupotet and was moved to repeat some of the experiments upon his boy. " Last night, as Mr Hewitt and I were sitting together, I called Henry in. He had never heard of the startling effects, and did not know what I was doing. After an operation of about five minutes, during the whole of which time he was laughing to himself at the absurd looking manipulations, his head suddenly declined, and he was quite asleep ! I had difficulty in wakening him. Here there could be no fancy, and he is a remarkably wakeful boy." " On Wednesday last (April 8, 1839) I went with Alfred Wornum to see Dr Elliotson's mesmeric experiments at the Dr's own house. The meeting was held in the drawing-room. . . . The Countess of Blessington came, and sat down quite close to me during some of the time. The things shown were truly wonderful. Let any sceptic go there, and if he be not *shaken* in his disbelief, the scepticism belongs to the will and not to the intellect."

He attended also a course of lectures by Thomas Carlyle in the summer of 1838. The two men were acquainted, possibly by Wilkinson writing to him his appreciation of this course of lectures. Three letters only from Carlyle were found among Dr Wilkinson's papers, but of these the two later indicate some intimacy.

c

"5 Cheyne Row, Chelsea,
"*August 2nd* 1838.

" Dear Sir,—Accept my best thanks for your gift of Em. Swedenborg's work, and for the kind sentiments you entertain towards me. That an earnest fellow-man recognizes an earnest meaning in us, and with brotherly heart wishes us success in our special course of endeavour : this is a true benefit, one of the truest and purest we can receive in this world. Alas, each man, enveloped in his own peculiarities and confused tortuosities, is in great part hidden from all men : seen only of the maker of men ! It is much if we can discern, here and there, darkly as thro' tumults and vapour, that here also is a brother struggling whither we struggle ; and call to him from the distance, ' Good speed to thee also ! '

" Hitherto I have known nearly nothing of Swedenborg ; or indeed I might say less than nothing, having been wont to picture him as an amiable but inane visionary, with affections quite out of proportion to his insight ; from whom nothing was to be learned. It is so we judge of extraordinary men. But I have been rebuked already : a little book by one Sampson Reed, of Boston in New England, which some friend sent hither, taught me that a Swedenborgian might have thoughts of the calmest sort on the deepest things, that in short I did *not* know Swedenborg, and ought to be ready to know him.

"I hope to find due leisure for studying this Book of yours before many days. I engage to read it with my best attention. Meanwhile, soliciting a continuance of your good will, I remain, dear Sir, yours with thanks,   T. CARLYLE."

The following long quotation in a letter to his *fiancée* from Garth Wilkinson is dated October 3, 1839 :—

"You may recollect that I sent a small packet to our friend Carlyle, containing 'Blake,' my translation of the 'Last Judgment,' Sampson Reed etc. On Saturday night, quite contrary to all my expectations, I received such a very kind brotherly letter from him! You will be pleased to see it. I have only copied what he says of Swedenborg. He speaks of me and my presents—then of Blake's 'Songs' and Preface—then he says :—

"'The book of Swedenborg's which you have translated anew, I read carefully in the old version received from you long ago. The impression it left was, and is, very strange. In his feeling about the *moral essence* of things, properly the core of his own being, I almost altogether and even emphatically agreed with him. It was clear, too, that he was a man of robust, nay, you would have said, cold, hard, practical-looking understanding : how such a man should have shaped for himself, into quiet historical concretions, standing there palpable, visible, solid and composed as the mountain rocks or more so, spiritual objects which eye hath not seen nor ear heard ; this is what I cannot at all put together.   I have looked into all the lives of Swedenborg that my Biographical Dictionaries would yield me ; but with little help there.   I ought to admit that this is one of the most wondrous men ; whom *I* cannot altogether undertake to interpret for myself !   I can love and honour such a man, and leave the mystery of him mysterious.'

"That good may go with you on the good path you travel so prays heartily, my dear Sir, yours always,   T. CARLYLE."

It will be convenient to deal here with the rest of this acquaintance, though the following notes are of a far later date than the time with which we are now dealing.   No doubt the second European visit of their common friend, Mr Emerson, had drawn the two men nearer together.

The first note is to decline an invitation to the wedding of Garth Wilkinson's eldest daughter Emma to Lieutenant Hermann Pertz.   It is interesting as showing Carlyle's struggle through the three last volumes of his " Frederick the Great."

" June 6th, 1859.

" MY DEAR SIR,—I am sorry to be cut off from attending you on this pleasant occasion. We are too weak here (especially the poor wife), and too busy (especially the other party, who is like to be swallowed and extinguished altogether with a job too heavy for him, and too hideous)—too weak and busy for going out at all, for many months past, even under the handiest circumstances.

" I pray you offer my respects and congratulations to all the parties, old and young, concerned in this glad business, and believe me, yours sincerely,

T. CARLYLE."

In the last note preserved (dated November 10, 1863) the struggle continues : it has visibly affected the handwriting and induced abbreviations.

" DEAR WILKINSON,—The Photograph is excell^t— very like ; and I am greatly obliged to you for it. We have put it into the brother compartment in the general Galaxy of friendly Faces ; and from time to time it will turn up as a memento, or be sought for as such, bringing nothing but pleasant thoughts with it.

" As to the Chelsea Photographs you speak of, I am far too busy to spare even an hour for such operations at pres^t : but surely in not many months

now my doleful Prussian (ultra - Babylonish)
Captivity will end; after wh[h], if permitted,
how happy shall I be to remember y[r] flattering
suggestion !

" Wish, for my sake, it may be soon.—Yours always
truly,   T. CARLYLE."

In March 1839, Garth Wilkinson had a serious
illness which laid him by for some weeks and this
was followed by a convalescence at Hampstead.
Later in the same year one of his sisters living with
him had small-pox : when it is interesting to notice
that the young householder lost no time in obtaining
lymph and vaccinating all the inmates and himself.
His fierce opposition to the process and its enforce-
ment was a growth of later date.

During these years of early practice, or rather
of waiting for practice and matrimony, impatience
was excusable. The young people even exerted
themselves, and tried to stir up influence, to obtain
an appointment as Veterinary Surgeon in India.
Fortunately Garth Wilkinson's uncle, Mr Sewell,
head of the Veterinary College, had a hatred of
nepotism and declined to move in the matter.

Mr Gaskell, a relative, was part proprietor of
the *Weekly True Son* and it seems likely that a
proposal was made that Wilkinson should become
a contributor and that the proposal was embraced,
though nothing of his writing has been traced there.

He projected an article on Swedenborg for the *Westminster Review*; but the idea stood over for the time, though it was not abandoned : for in 1842 he wrote the article " A sketch of Swedenborg and the Swedenborgians," for the " Penny Cyclopædia," which was reprinted as a booklet, and was doubtless the nucleus of his " Emanuel Swedenborg, a biography " published in 1849 and issued in a second amended edition in 1886.

The long time of waiting came to an end, and John James Garth Wilkinson was married to Emma Anne Marsh on January 4, 1840. Their income was small; their prosperity depended, humanly speaking, on their own exertions. But they were a couple who were ready to leave a large margin to faith. He, indeed, was not careful to be " too thoroughly justified " by worldly possessions in this momentous step ! They repaired straight from the church to their little house in Store Street, and began at once the homely unpretentious life which they designed to continue.

Let it be said at once that Garth Wilkinson was highly and deeply blessed in his married life. Destined never to be rich, he gained a wife whose deep fund of contentment and housewifely competence would have gilded means narrower than theirs. Eclectic and independent in the unpopular causes which he espoused, he found a mate who could trust the wisdom and sincerity of his aims ;

she could, moreover, understand and share them : subject as he was to those misgivings and apprehensions which at times beset the most enthusiastic, she brought an innate serenity of temperament into the partnership. They held together the highest principles, their qualities and powers were largely complementary. How far she made possible the tale of work which stands to his name, he and she alone knew ; and it was her constant aim to conceal her share in it. They remained, and doubtless still remain, true lovers.

We must not dwell on this subject at length ; but any account of Garth Wilkinson's life which did not acknowledge a debt, both in happiness and achievement, to his wife would be incomplete.

The visible fruit of this union was three daughters and a son ; we shall meet with allusions to them from time to time.

Garth Wilkinson's standing task after, as before, his marriage was the translation of the " Regnum Animale," but he found time for occasional articles for the *Monthly Magazine*, then edited by his friend Mr John A. Herraud. In November, 1840, he contributed a long and reasoned review of the whole subject of mesmerism, with which we deal later (see page 74). In May 1841, he collaborated with the editor in an article upon Emanuel Swedenborg, the first of three popular biographical accounts in which he was to be concerned. In the course

of the same year he contributed a criticism of certain
manuscript notes by S. T. Coleridge, found by Mr
Tulk in a copy of Swedenborg's " Œconomia Regni
Animalis." The writer points out that Coleridge's
comments were intelligible to a large body of students,
while the subjects of them belonged to an unknown
system, and were placed at an unfair disadvantage
by isolation from their contexts : he shows that
the critic read only the last fifth of the book and that
his annotations were written *passim*, and not upon a
calm consideration of all that he did read. Coleridge,
in his "inordinate lust of annotations," was as
it were, talking to himself as he read, and he was
used rather hardly in being himself criticized keenly
but politely : but the occurrence gave an opening
for Garth Wilkinson to champion and explain his
master, such an opening as he was not likely either
then, or later, to pass by.

One of these articles caught the eye and attracted the admiration of Mr Henry James, editor
of a Fourierist newspaper, *The Harbinger* of New
York, himself a polished writer upon theological
and metaphysical subjects, the father of Professor William James and of Mr Henry James,
the well-known writers of to-day. Notice led to
acquaintance, and acquaintance ripened into intimate friendship. For many years the two men
corresponded regularly, copiously and affectionately.
The letters from London to New York have been

carefully preserved, and give us a journal of the
intellectual occupations of the writer : those from
New York to London have been unfortunately
with few exceptions destroyed.

The new friend proved practically helpful as well
as intellectually suggestive and sustaining. Either
he or his wife, a woman whose modest charm of
manner and personal beauty made her everywhere
remarkable, dropped the seed which led Garth
Wilkinson to embrace homœpathy. This, as we
have already seen, reconciled him to the practice
of his profession, though it alienated him in great
measure from the bulk of his brother practitioners.
The new friend threw the columns of his own paper
open to a writer who had yet to make a name ; he
named him, when an English writer was wanted, as
weekly correspondent for the *New York Tribune*,
another journal of Fourierist tendencies, founded
by Horace Greely and edited by George Ripley,
who remained a life-long friend to Wilkinson. He
introduced him to the leading Americans who
visited England ; Emerson, Longfellow, Dana,
Hawthorne and many others were friends whom
Garth Wilkinson owed primarily to Mr James'
influence. But, more than this, he initiated and
fostered the acceptance and good repute of Wilkinson's work amongst the numerous adherents of
the New Church in the United States. There, even
more than here, the English interpreter of Sweden-

borg was widely and carefully read : and when, in 1869, he took a long contemplated but swiftly performed tour in America, he found his own name a passport to recognition and hospitality wherever he laid his foot.

The following extracts from a letter to one of his sisters (August 11, 1840), the only one of this period which has survived, gives some idea of his activities. After apologies for delay, he says " In the first place I have been busy for some weeks ; that is, relatively busy ; so that I have not been able, on many days, to apply myself to my translation, which you know generally goes on athwart almost everything. Then, in the next, I have been occupied rather more than was agreeable in writing and supervising the publication of the Report of *the* Printing Society ; which, however, is happily now *out*. . . . On Sunday week I was invited to Dr Elliotson's, to meet the Reverend Channey Hare Townshend, and to see some mesmeric experiments. . . . Amongst them (the guests) were Mr Tulk, Mr Townshend, Mr Dickens (Boz), Jack Forster and about 8 others. . . . Our life, though not a very uncomfortable (!), is a very unvaried one. Mine consists almost entirely in seeing what patients I have to see, and in writing two quarto pages *per diem*, winding up the day, now and then, by a call from a friend."

Garth Wilkinson had joined the Swedenborgian Society soon after he began the study of the writings, and it naturally was not long before he became a prominent member. He was on the Printing Committee which was engaged in bringing out a uniform edition of all the " Works " : there was some difference of opinion on the importance of this matter, and letters of an earlier date give a lively account of party politics in the Society. The Wilkinsons, for Garth was seconded by his brother William, now a rising solicitor, appear to have had at least a fair share of the direction. Wilkinson, as we shall see, was little in sympathy with the sectarian side of Swedenborgianism. He was concerned rather with the spiritual and intellectual side of the matter, and, in general, where essentials were not involved, gave his time to interpreting and translating the works.

His translation of the " Regnum Animale " was duly published in 1843, prefaced by a long and carefully written introduction. He demonstrates the scientific value of Swedenborg's work and presses his claims for recognition upon the scientists of the day. Incidentally he gives a disquisition upon the earlier anatomists, to show how fully his author was abreast of, or even ahead of, contemporary knowledge. Such an *excursus* argues special study. It is, indeed, evident that at this period of his life, Wilkinson was storing his mind with that vast knowledge which later showed itself in copious careless allusion in his published writings, his letters and his conversation.

He signalized the completion of this task by the first real holiday which he had taken since he began practice. In September 1843 he visited Brussels, Antwerp, Amsterdam and Leyden, seeing much that was new to him on his first Continental trip, and enjoying himself vastly; though with many a backward look to his wife and children at home.

After this brief interlude, he set himself down to the translation of the " Œconomia Regni Animalis." Nominally he was acting as editor of a translation formerly made by his friend the Reverend A. Clissold, but the labour which he expended upon it amounted to a re-translation. This, too, was prefaced by a long and thoughtful Introduction. But during the course of this, the second of Wilkinson's " monumental " translations, he found time to deliver a lecture on " The Grouping of Animals."

" Yesterday [1] I thought of you and your New York Lectures and your anticipatory trepidation; for last night I gave the first lecture I ever delivered ; and not without pain. It was before the Veterinary Medical Association, by request of that body. The audience was considerable, and comprised several scientific men of good repute, among the rest, Erasmus Wilson, the author of a good book on Anatomy. I chose for my subject the Grouping of Animals according to the Doctrine of Use, as

[1] Letter to Mr Henry J. James, May 17, 1845.

contradistinguished from the classification according to the race of external resemblances or uniformity; and aimed to show that the Domestic Animals were the head of the Zoological scale, in opposition to the monkeys. I flung out at the latter beasts, and the beastly hypotheses connecting them with man, with as much directness as I could: and did not mince the matter that science itself is but a servant, and must not be tolerated out of its place. The thing was well received, and will be published by and by."

Other works which marked this busy period were the writing of "Remarks on Swedenborg's 'Economy of the Animal Kingdom,'" 1846, some criticism of the big work which he had last translated; an edition of Swedenborg's "Opuscula" in their original Latin, 1846, followed the next year by a translation of the same entitled "Posthumous Tracts now first translated from the Latin of Emanuel Swedenborg"; a translation of "A Hieroglyphic Key to natural and spiritual mysteries by way of representations and correspondences" by the same author, 1847; an edition of Swedenborg's "Œconomia Regni Animalis," in its original Latin, 1847; a translation of Swedenborg's "Prodromus Philosophiæ Ratiocinantis de Infinito," under the title "Outlines of a Philosophical Argument on the Infinite, and the Final Cause of Creation, and on the Intercourse between the Soul and the Body,"

1847; and "a Popular Sketch of Swedenborg's Philosophical Works" 1847. In 1847 he also delivered a lecture upon Swedenborg's scientific works before the Swedenborgian Association, and published it under the title of "Science for All."

Only those who have carried through literary undertakings can recognize how much of labour such a catalogue represents. Let it be remembered, too, that many of these works were designed to take, and succeeded in taking, a place among the classics of an intellectual and critical body.

Garth Wilkinson was largely concerned in the foundation of the Swedenborgian Association, being a member of the Provisional Council and also of a small sub-committee for preparing a draft Constitution and Bye-laws. He also at this time contributed a review of Clissold's "Principia" to the "New Church Advocate." "The line of thought rudely indicated in that article" he writes to a friend, "is at present running in my head, and I design, God willing, to follow it out at greater length hereafter, probably in papers or lectures for the Swedenborgian Association."

It is clear that at this time, not only was Wilkinson willing to undertake hard work, but also that every piece of work which he did opened up vistas of consequent labours, and that he was anxious to follow them all. He was, in fact, at this time working extremely hard; not, indeed, without receiving great appreciation from those whose praise was dear ; but without anything like proportionate contributions towards the support of his home. The increase of his practice was slow. And this is not surprising to those who know how much of his thought and energy were being expended in quite extra-professional channels.

Among other plans which he entertained for the improvement of his condition was that of emigrating to America. This idea dated back as far as his acquaintance with Mr James, who was greatly in its favour. Inquiries were pushed on both sides of the Atlantic, but they ended in a recognition that the step was one of grave uncertainty, and the cherished thought was laid aside. "When my labours above mentioned (the translation of the 'Economy of the Animal Kingdom') are concluded," he writes to Mr James, at the end of 1844, "I shall think very seriously of America. We both wish to go to your country, both for the sake of our family, and in order that we may have a freer sphere of action : and if I had any certainty to go to, (which, I suppose, is impossible) I should not be long in deciding. . . . I entreat, however, that you will from time to time give us a hint on this subject of emigration, which is one that we shall not cease to keep before us."

A year and a half later, he refers to the subject, writing to the same friend :—

" I tell you plainly that if I were placed in any
responsible and satisfying position, by any joint
effort on the part of the admirers of Swedenborg
in America, the best of my mind and life should be
devoted to their service. . . . There is not, to
my knowledge, a thing under the moon that I
would rather choose to be connected with, were
it ' fancy's sketch ' that I were outlining. A small
fixed income—at any rate for a period; a cottage
out of New York, where my labours might mainly
be carried on; for, between ourselves, I am so
sick of this *tourbillon* of a city, and of all cities, that
it would be a blessing to me to live for a few years
rather further out than suburbs : labours connected
with the literature and philosophy of Swedenborg :
and association with those who sympathize with
my pursuits; for I have *no* such association here ;
no, not a single voice to say, *go on*. . . . All
these conditions fill up something which I should,
nay do, desire with might and main ; and which,
if it be right, I do not doubt of attaining."

The freedom and diversity of the American people
and conditions were a constant tractor to him,
during these years. His foresight in the following
extract from a letter, has been abundantly justified.

" Your futurity promises to be great beyond
what History has to show in the past; that is to
say, if your souls are equal to your chances. A
climate ranging from the temperate to the torrid

D

zone, and peopled by the *genera* of all civilized, and
nearly all uncivilized, mankind, is a composition
of circumstances which, when united to the fact
that the whole rest of the world calls upon you
to be useful to them, must give you wealth and
variety to a surprising degree. It sometimes seems
to me that it would be no pusillanimous flight from
my poor position here, to go to help on with my
feeble arm the youthful pursuits of a nation destined
to be so provisive for old England, as well as for
the entire world."

But in May, 1849, the advices of Mr James, cor-
roborated by those of another American friend,
finally determined all hopes and anticipations of an
emigrational nature.

In following briefly this part of Wilkinson's
correspondence with Mr James we have left un-
recorded certain matters of varying importance.

In 1847, it was found that the better part of
the doctor's patients lived in and around Hampstead.
He therefore sold the remainder of his lease of 13
Store Street and followed them thither, settling
in more congenial quarters, at 25 Church Row—a
neighbourhood much more definitely suburban then
than now, but his residence there was not to be
a long one.

In 1848, Ralph Waldo Emerson paid his second
visit to Europe and brought with him an introduction
to Garth Wilkinson in the handwriting of Mr James.

The two men were already known to each other by
their works, and they were not slow in forming a
warm and stable friendship. Emerson was already
well read in Swedenborg and this new acquaintance
increased his interest in the writings : it would
be interesting to know how far the lecture upon
" Swedenborg, or the Mystic " was completed when
Emerson arrived in England, how much was added
and what modifications it underwent, during his
stay here.

Mrs Wilkinson was away from home during
Emerson's visit to London, a fact to which we owe
some letters mentioning meetings with him.

" I am going to spend the evening with Dr
Carpenter," he writes on April 4, 1848, " to meet
Emerson, where I shall also see Daniel Morell and
other friends. I find Emerson has been speaking
warmly of me."

On April 10, he records : " Our party came off
last night, and altho' everyone said they felt so
strange at the absence of Mrs Wilkinson, and Mr
Emerson particularly regretted it, as ' he had counted
upon seeing you,' yet we made the best of it, and
shone away as fiercely as we could, like despairing
stars when the moon is out. I went in the gig for
Emerson at half past 3, and brought him up to
Williams', where we sat and chatted and walked
round the farm ; then walked to the Heath by the
fields, and enjoyed a most friendly and interesting

chat. . . . Emerson delighted me and everybody.
I must say, he grows upon my regard exceedingly."

On the 17th he dined with friends and met Emerson
and Crabb Robinson. "The said Crabb Robinson
is one of the most entertaining and interesting old
gentlemen I ever met. He is one of the Council
of University College, an old friend of Mr Tulk's
and one of the executors of Flaxman. He knew
Blake well. After tea, he singled me out by miracle,
and entertained me beyond measure about the
great artist. It was he who gave Blake 25 guineas
for the 'Songs of Innocence.' He warmly invited
me to call upon him, when he will show me several
of Blake's originals, both poems and pictures."

Emerson has been called "the sanest of the
Transcendentalists" but he was distinctly a distinguished and discriminating Transcendentalist;
and everybody who has considered transcendentalism
is prepared to recognize Garth Wilkinson as a member
of the same brotherhood. Emerson at all events
recognized him at sight, and, as we shall shortly see,
was ready to help him, not only with valuable literary
encomium, but also with personal recommendations
as a lecturer. It is not too much to say that his
influence at a critical time was a predominant
factor in gaining for his friend a literary, social
and professional recognition which he then greatly
needed and which he thereafter constantly justified
and improved. Emerson gave the " word in season "

which was wanted : Wilkinson had the power to seize the forelock of opportunity.

Wendell Holmes, in his interesting but unsatisfying biography of Emerson, names "two notable products of the intellectual ferment of the Transcendental period "; *The Dial* periodical and Brook Farm. Wilkinson's literary work and ideals were closely parallel to those of *The Dial*, though he was never a contributor to that paper. He was now to give his mind to the "true begetter" of the Brook Farm ideal. In America, Brook Farm, begun enthusiastically upon lines even less definite, developed into a determined attempt to carry out the idea of Fourier in a working "Phalanstery." An experiment of six years (1841-1847) ended to all intent in the destruction of the settlement by fire. Like all the contemporary efforts to realize Fourier's ideals, it was a failure.

Fourier, who was born in 1772 and died in 1837, has shared the fate of many idealists. His purely abstract views of human nature and social possibilities have hindered the acceptance of certain excellent and concrete proposals for the benefit of society. He lived before the world was ready for him; his Socialistic message contained some glaring fallacies and many wild words : his immediate followers "eat the air, promise-crammed"; he himself died the lonely death of a pioneer. His name is unfamiliar alike to the small shareholder

in the Co-operative Stores and to the member of Trade
Unions, both of whom taste the fruit of his labours,
now that the tree has been pruned out of recognition
and adapted to " common or garden " culture.

There was some pressure upon Wilkinson to become a Fourierist. Social problems never seemed
more urgent for solution than they did at this time ;
when the power of aristocracy had waned, only to
be succeeded by the power of a dominant middle
class. Speculation and theory were busy among the
Intuitionists ; the strength of the Utilitarians had
not yet shown itself. It was a fit time for doctrines
such as those of Fourier, St Simon and Owen to
gain adherents. Moreover, Mr James' paper, *The
Harbinger*, was the quasi-official organ of Brook
Farm : Emerson was keenly sympathetic to the
movement, though he was never a Brook-farmer
himself. It was likely that Wilkinson should examine
Fourier for himself. We can trace the result in his
correspondence, though it is scarcely necessary that
this should always be quoted at length.

At first Fourier definitely repelled his student,
who found his writings arrogant, pugnacious, given
to *petitio principii*, impudent. The man himself
appeared to be without a central religious faith :
lacking this, he fails of his intended function as a
great scientist : having it, his powerful perception
of the *universal mathematics* of the sciences might
have raised him high indeed : his experience is small

in quantity and poor in quality : and Doctrine
without experience is useless. Six months later
(August 1846) we find the note changing, and the
reason for the change is given to us. Dr Hugh
Doherty " is marrying Fourier to the New Church,
giving the former, however, the masculine character
in the compact." Fourier's analysis of the twelve
Passions seems eminently valuable as leading direct
to the organization of the Sciences." A few months
later the process of conversion is clearly going on.
In June 1, 1847, Wilkinson finds it natural that
Fourierism should attract attention in America,
" for the whole thing is *jolly human* "; moreover
the Fourierists have a more tangible belief in immortality and in the interdependence of the spiritual
and natural worlds than any body of people except
the Swedenborgians. Six weeks later he writes
" All you say of the Association movement I echo
from my heart. It is *the* morning brightness of the
world's day." He is reviewing a book by his friend
John Morell which deals with the subject, and will
procure a copy for *The Harbinger*.

An extract from a letter written to Mr James
on October 1, 1847, will show how fully Fourier
had by that time found himself a place as at least
an accessory to Swedenborg in Wilkinson's consideration—" What I have at present on the stocks
for you is a paper on Correspondences, which I
trust will be finished before the middle of this month,

and sent, if possible, by the steamer of the 19th. It will treat the subject as a branch of the movement, and not sink it in the mere laudation of Swedenborg. First, I attempt to show that the doctrine, as a general idea, is common to all men upon the least thought : Secondly, that the working out of the Doctrine supposes a vast science, and not a set of guesses arising from preconceived ideas : Thirdly, that in the happier times, this science will be the crown of the sciences, from its intensely practical character ; because correspondence is the circumstance which draws down the spiritual world into nature, and engenders Creations according to the disposition of the lower world. I am not without hopes that the Paper may be useful, and prepare some to carry forward the views of Swedenborg and Fourier, instead of being, as heretofore, the mere turnspits of those central fires."

On February 11, 1848, Wilkinson writes to Mr James to sympathize with him under an attack by *The Boston Magazine* upon an article which had evidently associated " those central fires." He is not surprised, since the standpoint is not easily grasped, and also because he ventures to doubt whether Mr James had himself sufficiently formulated his position as mediator between the Truths of Swedenborg and the Truths of Fourier. He himself is of opinion that the mission of Fourier had better be worked out for some time to come, say for a quarter of a century, on its own grounds, separately from dogmatic theology. When the theologians see Fourierism at work, if it does work, they will not dare to despise or denounce it. He is not confident that the time for Association has yet come.

This temporizing attitude was fully justified by experience. Swedenborgianism has had quite enough to do without dragging the extravagances of Fourier behind it. It must not be forgotten, either, that Fourier's doctrine, as crudely stated by him, contemplated a period in which the natural passions would play unbridled. This stage, which would clearly have made practical adherents of the doctrine unwelcome in every civilized community, was wisely regarded as unnecessary at Brook Farm, and was generally ignored. Union with a system, which, even in theory, could be connoted with " Free Love " was impossible for any Christian Church.

Writing to Mr Emerson to bespeak his kindly consideration for the Reverend J. R. Morell's translation of Fourier " On the Soul " (a work, by the way, in which he himself had given more than occasional help) Wilkinson says " I look upon Fourier as the first worthy historian of the Animal Man," an expression which epitomises the results of his Fourieristic studies sufficiently well. We may date back to these studies some of the fierceness with which he attacked everything which bore the semblance of undue State interference with the individual. Compulsory Vaccination, the Contagious Diseases Act, state qualifications in medicine, probably owe some of the sting in his lash to the intense individualism which Fourier fostered.

Ordinary holiday travel is apt to lose its salt in transcription ; but there were conditions which make Dr Wilkinson's first visit to Paris in 1848, interesting, even to-day. In England, either by good luck or good management, the Chartist rising had not culminated in revolution : but there was a general uneasy feeling that it was only the first wave of a storm which had broken. There was trouble throughout Europe. The wave of democratic action swept over nearly every government, and nowhere more suddenly or fiercely than in France. As he himself wrote on his return [1] :—

" That visit is still engraven on me, and comes out in dream and reverie with singular vividness. Nothing would be more profitable to me than to travel over Europe just now : Volcanic countries present the most striking as well as often beautiful pictures, and pictures are the skins and costumes of the soul. But really in England too we may likely have movement soon ; the hush and excessive triviality of politics, the silence so deep that fine sounds are heard upon it, betoken a coming storm. All the cattle, too, are flying to shelter,

[1] Letter to Mr Henry James, New York, July 28, 1848.

under those large old trees which may first call down
the lightning. Their very instincts are wrong at
such a time. In a word, England too is profoundly
sub-volcanic. The finest vineyards are growing
upon it, within a few feet, and even in consequence
of, the terranean sulphor."

When it was possible almost to hear the storm
sing in the wind around the house, the sight of a
neighbour actually suffering it was absorbing in
interest. His brother William had just returned
from a visit to Paris, full of what he had seen and
heard. Garth felt that he could not remain at
home, while such sights and sounds were within
reach. With several friends, he started for Paris
about June 2nd and joined his old friend Dr Doherty
and Lord Wallscourt. A letter dated June 25th
tells of his being in the centre of what was going on :—

" Here we are, much tired, but quite safe and well :
we arrived at this place through sundry obstacles,
but none really serious. It is a splendid city,
but a day of horrors. Yesterday, by cannonad-
ing and musketry no less than 25,000 souls
perished : nothing like it since the last Revolution,
or since the Massacre of St Bartholomew. Two
thousand men of the working class were butchered
in the vaults of the Pantheon, which was ankle-
deep in it. The Musketry has not ceased all night,
and it is interrupted every now and then by heavy
Artillery. But we are, I assure you, perfectly safe

and I would not have missed the events for the
world. They are historical. You can have no
idea of them."

Later he wrote :—

" The fusillade and cannonade lasted all yesterday,
and as I was philosophically reading Doherty on
the Series this morning, about half past two (I had
waked up for an hour), the *coups de canon* recom-
menced, and that and the musketry kept up very
audibly at intervals till this morning. Now I
understand that the greater part of the Barricades
have been taken, excepting those of the Faubourg
St Antoine where the troopers have not yet been
able to penetrate. . . . We have been walking
about near the Tuileries and Louvre, watching
the forests of bayonets as they stream towards
the Faubourg St Antoine, where the rough work
is to be done. . . . The Churches are full of the
dead, and all the women are sitting at the doors,
making *charpie* for the wounded. Every now and
then we see them being brought into the Ambulances.
The whole is a scene of Devilry on a magnificent
scale, as I can never hope to see again. . . . As to
my personal adventures, I shall probably write and
tell you them when we return. They have been
amusing enough, but you could scarcely understand
them without a commmentary. Be assured, however,
that they belong to Comedy, not Tragedy. . . .
You can have no idea of what French pluck is :

it is all, and more than all, of what Irish talk is : and that is a good deal. In fact there are in Paris hundreds of thousands who dare to die at any moment. To see them is to me a lesson in human nature. I did not know that there were such spiritual beings, such ready-made ghosts. They brave death because they are already spirits to the finger ends, and their steel is immortal. There are in Paris about 500,000 men under arms and fresh troops are pouring in from the country every hour. Only imagine the spectacle presented in every street, alive as it is with red cloth, glitter-ing *fusils* and bayonets. But it is a sight that I hardly wish you to see."

" The insurrection is crushed. . . . The streets are becoming more free, and last night Doherty and I perambulated the Quays, to see the moving life. The troops passed us, flushed with the affair of the Faubourg St Antoine. . . . The cruellest thing of all was the Government putting forward the poor little Gardes Mobiles into the thick of the battle, to fight against their brother *ouvriers*. An officer told us last night, that out of one battalion of a thousand, but fifty men were left in service."

" The prisoners are now being brought in, escorted by masses of bayonets. Many are lads with fine intelligent faces : they have their hands tied behind their backs, and march in the midst of the troops with a sad, heroic air. It is one of the most melancholy sights that the world presents; intelligent, brave hunger, compressed and crushed by the bayonets of the upper Classes."

" I send you Wallscourt's letter just received. He, like ourselves, has heard the *whizz* of iron near his precious head. It is an exciting *siffle*, but only alarming when you are about three hundred miles off it."

" So ends the first skirmish between Socialism and the old civilization. . . . Judging the beginning of Socialism by the beginning of Liberal Politics, how vast is the preponderance of force in favour of the former ! "

" We have seen the battle streets, and instructed ourselves thereby . . . and seen a sight for a lifetime : all the appearance of a city taken by storm. . . . But, after all, the most memorable part was the fierce imprint left by the fight. Barricades everywhere, and the houses riddled and smashed and crushed with hail of musketry and deadly strokes of cannon. You can't conceive it. On one house 14 feet square the indefatigable Phillips counted 482 musketry hits and 9 cannon shots. . . . We took a cab and drove to other interesting things of the moment. First we saw the funeral of General Negrier, whose remains were borne in a rich car, ornamented with spears and tricolours. But the best sight of the day was the Archbishop of Paris. Noble fellow ! there he lay, in his palace, in his room of state, hung with sables, adorned with his insignia, and reclining upon a sloping couch, for all the world like a good spirit sleeping till to-morrow's work. Really, the French are great Cooks; and whether it is a Procession, or an ovation, or a chop, or a *cadavre*, they get it up, and engraft upon it a second nature of beauty and refinement, in a style quite striking for me. Death has none of his terrors when they polish him off! "

" Paris is illuminated every night, in order to make the streets as light as possible and prevent a certain system of popping which goes on when we are abed, after 11 o'clock : before that hour the daily shooting season has not commenced ; but, after that, the sentinels are fair game, and we may (if not asleep) hear the crying out all night with admirable distinctness. *Gardez bien a vous*; the *vous* very loud. . . . No passage during the night is allowed near or behind them, but all must keep the mid road. . . . There goes the everlasting *rappel* and the measured tread, past the Tuileries."

" What I have seen convinces me of this. The Parisians care no more about life than we do about a few coppers, and they are not susceptible of fear for any length of time, but it will be converted into untamable rage. It is a sad state of things ; but Providence is over all, working out His great designs of Peace through the passions of hostile nations, and making their wrath praise Him."

" We have just seen the Funeral Pomp of the Victims of June. . . . 'Twas a grand military spectacle, an immense piece of Cookery."

There were naturally other and more normal sights in a first visit to Paris. Enghien, Montmorenci and Versailles, the sewage works at Montfaucon, the Abattoir and so forth were visited. But from the account of such doings we will cull only one extract as recalling an almost forgotten name, that of Robert Owen, the successful cotton-spinner who later nigh upon beggared himself as an experimental Socialist, the founder of Communities at New Lanark, Ratahine and Tytherly. He died ten years later, but too early to see many of his ideas developed in practice.

" Last night we had a curious party ; Brisbane, Phillips, Daly, Doherty, Dana, Wallscourt and Robert Owen. Old Owen is lodging in this house ; he is a nice quiet old citizen of the world, wedded most amusingly to his circumstances and parallelograms, and, for the rest, putting his conceit aside, a humble enough specimen of a man. He always thinks that the morrow is to see Owenism prevalent over the world, and that all his failures have been successes. There is something in a man who has received a life of stripes and still does not know that he is beaten."

It is evident that as much experience and novelty as possible was concentrated into a brief holiday before Garth Wilkinson returned to "England, home and duty" on the sixth of July.

Practice not satisfying the requirements of his growing family, and all thought of settling in America being over, it was necessary that Wilkinson should supplement his means by some extra-professional work. And this suited well with his propagandist zeal for the doctrines of Swedenborg. This was a time when, in Brougham's words, "the schoolmaster was abroad": philosophy was also peripatetic. The Society for the Diffusion of Useful Knowledge, and the Mechanics' Institutes which existed and flourished in almost every town, testify to a keen thirst for information; no doubt the supply and the demand mutually stimulated each other. Certainly the lecture was a popular road to knowledge (or, at least, to superficial information) about the "thirties," "forties," and "fifties" of the last century. The man who had anything to say, or any views to indoctrinate, could not do better than lecture his fellow-creatures. It was an avenue to the public ear which Thackeray, Dickens, Carlyle, and Emerson did not despise; and there were, it may safely be said, hundreds of lesser lights who illuminated their fellows and toured the larger towns of the country with a course of three or four lectures in their carpet-bags. The lecturer supplied the night's entertainment. A diagram or two, a few specimens, might be provided; but the magic

E

lantern and dissolving views were still unknown. There was, in fact, such a supply of lecturers that to find lucrative engagements in the best towns was not an easy matter; as Garth Wilkinson, having issued a syllabus for a course of lectures on the Physics of Human Nature, discovered. But he had a powerful ally in Mr Emerson, who had ready admittance to just those audiences which his less-known friend was anxious to address; and, wherever Mr Emerson lectured and elsewhere, there he dropped a germinal recommendation of Garth Wilkinson. We find him writing in acknowledgement.

[1] " I cannot tell you in the space of a letter how much your kind word has done for me in England, and in my own town. For a long time I could not understand the place which I seemed to occupy in the good feelings of many worthy and clever persons, but by slow degrees the truth dawned upon me, that *you* had done it all. It is even so, I assure you. What you may have said, I know not, and I do not wish to know; but this I do know, that the words, whatever they were, gained me a position that I had not before, and which seems to me unmerited by my deeds. Nay; the fruits have not been all opinions; but many a coin has run into my exchequer from the same stream of your kind expressions. And in a Lecture Tour, I found that you

[1] Letter to Mr R. W. Emerson, October 15, 1849.

had everywhere been there also, dropping your
charities from your own unique urn."

With such a powerful endorsement, the syllabus
took more prosperous journeys and was followed
often by the lecturer. His tours included the
Whittington Club (London), Liverpool, Manchester,
Birmingham, Derby, and Leeds. There was only
one accident worthy of record during these journeys.
Mr and Mrs Wilkinson returned from Liverpool
via Sheffield, and stayed there some days with a
friend, Mr Phillips. Driving with him in a pony
carriage, they were about to visit Montgomery
the poet (not "Satan" Montgomery, whom
Macaulay gibbeted, but James, author of "Pelican
Island" and many hymns) and pulled up at the top
of the hill. The pony bolted down the hill again.
The two gentlemen were thrown out, but Mrs
Wilkinson was carried sixty yards at full gallop.
They were all badly bruised, but were thankful
to escape alive. Garth Wilkinson "escaped almost
unhurt, which I take as a divine sign that I have
work to do yet, and that I am to use my energies
therefor."

The full syllabus of the six lectures on the Physics
of Human Nature, as delivered at the Liverpool
Mechanics' Institute on August 2, 1848, and on
each succeeding Saturday and Wednesday, shows
that they concerned themselves respectively with the
brain, the lungs, the heart, food and assimilation,

the skin, and the human form. In most places, however, the course appears to have consisted of either three or four lectures. Each lecture was in reality a demonstration, firstly, in elementary anatomy and physiology, secondly (and this was the important point in the lecturer's scheme), in the doctrine of correspondences : the powder of doctrine was conveyed in the jam of information. The line of thought was one which Wilkinson followed and produced, in more detail and to more purpose, later, when he wrote " The Human Body and its Connection with Man."

The reports given by the provincial press make this fairly evident, though it is amusing to notice how the true gist of the matter did not always attract attention.

" On Monday evening last Mr J. J. Garth Wilkinson delivered a lecture at the Mechanics' Institute on the Human Brain. Notwithstanding the extremely unfavourable weather, there was a numerous attendance. After some prefatory remarks, the lecturer explained, and illustrated by means of diagrams, some of the chief features in the anatomy of the brain. . . . Mr Wilkinson then contended that the animal spirit was formed in the cortex of the brain, and was impelled thence through the body by an automatic motion of the brain itself. He endeavoured to show that the brain respired at the same intervals with the lungs, but in a higher atmosphere, and in a more eminent degree. The manner in which these doctrines were settled decided the fate not only of physiology, but of philosophy. If there was no universal body living in the particular body, mankind had no communion with the universe, but was limited to solid sensualities. If there was no spirit in the nerves, man was not embodied at all, or else he was nothing but body; and in either of these cases, the general laws of nature were fixed hypotheses incapable of proof, or delusions to be abjured or forgotten. So we must wander between metaphysics and stupidity, between idealism and spiritualism, without daring to look our souls in their natural faces—a sad result, which could only be contravened by a knowledge and study of an animal spirit existing in the body. Mr Wilkinson was warmly applauded throughout and at the conclusion of his lecture, of which the above is only a slight sketch."—*Manchester Guardian*, Wednesday, October 11, 1848.

" . . . What then was the end in view of the process of digestion and assimilation ? In one sense, it was the formation of the blood ; but in a higher sense, it was that we might live in the world by means of a body derived from the world, and representing the world. To be completely men of nature, we required to be allied to her by our constitution, to marry into all her royal families, to take a body from every kingdom, in order that we might enter, inhabit, appreciate and understand it. The sense of taste, and the alimentary series which he had been considering, afforded us our lowest or material embodiment, by which we were brought into fellowship with the mineral, vegetable, and animal; the sense of smell and the pulmonary series, gave us our aerial food, by which we gained the freedom of the atmosphere; the brain was the governor of assimilation, realizing for the body all the æthers and spaces of the mundane system, and introducing man into all the elements of his being. The highest organization, as well as the lowest, was omnivorous, eating the whole universe. The lecturer concluded by some remarks on the psychology of digestion and assimilation in nature and society."—*Manchester Guardian*, Oct. 18, 1848.

" . . . While the action of the lungs in drawing the venous blood to the heart had been well canvassed, their action upon the great nerves and spinal marrow had not been thought of. The nerves were the most impressible part of the body; and what, could be the result of the expansion to which they were constantly subject, but the admission of a fluid along them large enough to fill the space created ? And must not this effect, in the same instant, amount to expansion of all the parts to which the nerves or fluid were sent—viz. to all the viscera of the frame ? Then the lungs not only breathed themselves, but caused the body to breathe with them. In the body there was an organic attraction, corresponding to that of the organic world, enabling all the organs to take what they wanted. These organs, too, were conveniently placed for this purpose; those needing the best blood being so seated at the banquet that they obtained what they required naturally and necessarily. They were classed in exact rank, each having its attraction, seconded by its place around the table. The order which this subject involved, could it be fully opened, would exceed the most hopeful conception and beggar the visions of the poets. If each organ, then, contributed its share to the *ensemble* of life, each demanded a special care in the maintenance of health, which was the wealth of life. (Here followed some strictures upon tight lacing.) If motion was the essence of the life of the organs, all our articles of apparel might fairly be supervised and limited in their pressure, in order that our persons might enjoy their healthful liberty. It was not to be doubted that in what we wear, equally as in what we are, grace, pleasure, and beauty are compatible with freedom, and with freedom only. The lecturer concluded by some remarks on the universality of the functions of breathing, or alternation in nature and society. He was frequently and warmly applauded throughout the lecture."—*Derby Mercury*, January 17, 1849.

Such was the impression which the lectures made at the reporters' table. What the lecturer felt meanwhile is told in a letter to Mr Henry James.[1]

"As soon as I get back to Hampstead, I will be less egotistic in my communications, and we will have a long chat upon our old subjects; at present I am so engrossed with my new travellings and altered mode of life, that I can hardly think of anything else.

"Everybody tells me that I shall in a little time have my winter full of lecturing, and become popular in that line. Certainly I feel in good heart at the prospect of usefulness which seems opening before me.

"I am now meditating a course on The Kingdom of Sleep. . . . I shall try to make it interesting to *you*, so do not think that I am going into any old catalogue work or copying from anybody.

"My last lecture (at Liverpool) was coldly received, but successful for all that. The audience and the lecturer seemed to me like two stones, trying which was the hardest; but I am sure that we parted good friends, or kind foes, whichever you like. I minced nothing, and my poor wife told me she shook all over to hear my strange heterodoxy so audible in the dead silence."

He wrote again in the same sense to the same friend (September 15, 1848). After mentioning

[1] August 25, 1848.

his existing engagements, he speaks of preparing other courses of lectures. His attitude is " to see the subjects all round ; to recognize the omnipresence of truth ; to believe in the travelling force of the great streams of God. For this purpose I despise nothing, but whatever be the subject, I first take its description, and note its stock ; then its plain uses ; then the divinity and history of the knowledge of it ; its representation and appearance in Mythology and Philosophy ; and what Poetry has said and still says to it ; then how it occurs in language, and lastly what is the peculiar view of it at this day ; and, gathering up these several informations, I next try to see them as forms and uses ; and conclude by carrying out the thing through a few of its analogies, in Society, History, Spirituality. . . . Even with my feeble powers, I find the method helpful to me, and attractive to the listeners. And the fields of fact which it opens are so immense and fruitful that one never thinks of controversies, but instead of them, one invites others to better arrangements of the facts ; calling forth, not criticism, but emulous works."

The projected new courses, as well as a scheme for publishing those which were actually delivered, in book form, were never realized ; but his method is worthy of being recorded, as he clearly followed it in other manifestations of work.

While he was lecturing in Manchester, Mr Wilkinson

was introduced to Mr James Braid, and was deeply interested in his practice of hypnotism. Mr Braid was not satisfied with the pretensions of magnetism; and, on experiment, he found that he could do all and more than those who followed it, though he dispensed with all their paraphernalia of magnets and crystals. Mr Braid's conclusions have long been generally adopted, but they then had all the charm of novelty, and, as reaching toward what is now called the subliminal consciousness, had a special attraction for Garth Wilkinson. He had already himself critically examined the claims of Mesmerism in an extended review for *The Monthly Magazine* (vol. iv. No. 23), and had expressed grave doubts of its utility for the patient, though he regarded it as opening up great possibilities in " pyschological analysis." The new development, and the elimination of the personal will factor from its processes, gave him a fresh zest in following out and examining the phenomena and theories of mental states.

We anticipate a little in giving here an extract from a letter [1] which illustrates Wilkinson's expectation of a new " influx " of power to the art of healing, from another aspect.

" The other evening I met at Mr A. I. Scott's (the Professor of English Literature at University College, London) a Mr Dillon Tennant, who represents a mode of curation novel in these roundabout ages.

[1] To Mr H. J. James, April 13, 1849.

He is a person of character and standing, and may be relied on. Whateley, the Archbishop of Dublin, has witnessed and investigated his cures, and I have seen his autograph papers attesting the facts. Mr Dillon Tennant was led in the first instance to these beneficences by seeing a friend in great torture, unrelieved by other means, and he was moved to say to himself : ' *In the name of God*, I'll mesmerize him.' He did so, and in a few minutes the pain was gone. After this he tried the same thing for many sufferers, always ' in the name of God,' and succeeded. . . . Each person so treated—and the operation sometimes proceeded at the rate of a cure *per* minute—he bent on his knees to give thanks to God. . . . Frequently from 50 to 100 persons were relieved at one *séance*. I am glad to have seen him, because he recalls to available knowledge certain old-fashioned Prophets and Apostles whom one too easily forgets. His, like theirs, appears to be the actual power of faith as an organ and a substance. I am not able, it is true, to place great stress upon his cases : I know too little of them ; but they send me to the Apostolical and Christian cures, which I do potentially believe ; and place before my eyes what I have long been looking for ; the Divine Stem of Healing ; that channel pipe which runs with panaceas ; and of which all medicine, in its varieties of systems, is but the branches. . . . There are arts better than ours ; machines and ways better than ours; and the world shows its Divine origin in being large enough to have GOD in it as well as man."

In June of this year (1849) Wilkinson began his duties as writer of a weekly letter for *The New York Tribune.* There are words which suggest that the task was not congenial, and it was relinquished in December 1850.

Meanwhile he found an important work to do for the New Church. He has got himself entangled, he says in a letter, in a life of Swedenborg, which had occupied all his time; it is going on very fast and he hopes that another fortnight will disburden him of it; he does it *con amore*, having long been preparing for it. He means to have it published also in the United States. He began it with the idea of a threepenny pamphlet in his mind; but it grew under his hand and formed a very complete biography, so far as the facts and their order are concerned. " I scarcely venture to hope that the Swedenborgians will like it, because I have not treated Swedenborg as either a *ne plus ultra* or an idol. It is not a philosophical or progressive affair —professedly; though I hope that it will disabuse worthy people of some of their falacies."

His expectations were more than realized, for the sectarian Swedenborgians did not like the book— indeed, they " vituperated " it; but worthy people who were seeking candid information on the subject

were otherwise minded. So much so that a new
and slightly amended edition was called for in
1860, and the book still has a public of its own.
The work of three hundred odd pages was completed
in three months.

We have seen that Wilkinson had been working
hard—harder probably than was wise—for some
years. For it must be remembered that he added
a growing quantity of medical work to the extraordinary literary output which stands to his credit.
There is little wonder, then, that the strain showed
itself at times in mental depression and bodily
weakness. Mr James had expressed some intention
of bringing his family to Europe for educational
purposes. In a letter encouraging this project
Wilkinson writes to him (August 6, 1849):
" Certainly this is a splendid climate for producing
healthful bodies, and a good thing too ; for the
quantity of work required of an Englishman is no
trifle. . . . Then, for a man like you, the Society
is ever varied, and the stimulation incessant. For
us, it is true, this is not so, for my ideas are merely
those of duty now ; I look on pleasure as impossible ;
and being like you (in ' Becky Sharp ') [1]—a man of
all the sins, I look for no fact but in that everlasting
work that crushes out self-thought every moment.
Prison and task-mastering are the blessings—the
vast blessings—of the day, and happy is he over whom

[1] A recent study of Thackeray's heroine, written by Mr James.

necessity stands with a rod of iron, feruling him for every moment not devoted to the most absorbing labour.   That is my creed for *myself*, and though I cannot contemplate it as an ultimate lot, yet I do feel that its only limit is the grave.   I am jolliest when I feel it most, and I make a creed of it, to have all artificial checks provided against rebellion."

Shortly before this he had written: "For a length of time now I have been hydropathizing, and with huge benefit to mind and body.   'Tis astonishing how much more work I can do, what absence of customary invitations I feel, under the *wishy-washy* régime.   Even when I am ill, I can still work on, and observe my *malaise* with a kind of upper mind, as though my sickness was . . . an instructive panorama."

Wilkinson was one of those men who required "a little wine for *his* stomach's sake," and his pessimism vanished speedily when he returned to his usual and very moderate potations.   But the experience left him sore against the ultra-teetotal school.   He wrote a long account of Carpenter's prize essay on Alcoholic Liquors, to Mr James, and concluded it as follows: "The human chemistry of the case, which lies in the union of emotions with wine, is therefore quite a different study from the animal chemistry.   And as this is a matter that is of very great importance for men's thoughts at present, I design to go into it in my labours, and to endeavour to develop a few sentences of a precise kind, on the subject of this unknown human chemistry. Certainly wine shall not be blasphemed in my hearing, without a strenuous effort to rescue it from peril." His defence of wine against the "blasphemies" of the intemperate temperance party duly appeared in *The Human Body* (pp. 168 *et seq.*).

During these years his dissatisfaction in the traditional practice of medicine had been growing in Wilkinson's mind. The doctrine of Hahnemann had been brought to his notice by Mr James, by Mrs Carter, another American friend, and by the general interest which followed the introduction of its practice into England by Dr Quin in 1837. He had read what works he could find on the subject, and had experimented in the treatment inculcated by them more and more extensively, until he must be regarded as a staunch Homœopath in 1850. His works, words, and ideas in this connection will best be considered in a separate chapter. But his conversion was an event in his life too important to be passed over without mention here; since, as we have seen, it reconciled him to practice and made him happy in it. His clientéle increased at once, and he must now be regarded from a changed point of view. Up to 1850, he was a writer, specializing upon theology from a Swedenborgian outlook, who practised physic for a maintenance; from that time forward he was a physician who found time to write upon the old subjects. Only two more translations from Swedenborg's writings came from his pen, and they were separated by an interval of more than thirty years.

Hitherto his medical and scientific knowledge had tinctured his work for the New Church. His vital interest in that Church never flagged: but we have now reached a period, and a long one, in which the interest seldom showed itself in his writings, except as illustrative of matters medical and scientific. This " second manner " lasted, indeed, until he virtually retired from practice; or, rather, encouraged practice to retire from him. But there was a transition period, and in it he produced what was, perhaps, of all his writings, the work most fully characteristic of the man.

This book, " The Human Body and its Connection with Man, illustrated by the Principal Organs," was a substitute for the publication of his lectures; but it represents those lectures as elaborated and enriched by the reflections of the author since they had been delivered. The first mention of it occurs in a letter to his father in July 1849; but a letter to Mr James, at the end of the same year, enters into more detail.

" This is the first work on which I at all stake myself, and I am proportionately anxious to put the last hand to it. On nothing else have I accumulated labour. And, as you are to be its patron saint,

I am particularly tremulous on your account also. The field is a new one—that of the Correspondences of the Human Frame; I do not mean the spiritual correspondences, but the continuations of it into nature, into industry, into society, and into mind. I feel that the physical man is the keystone of the arch of the arts, and that to open his truths, be it ever so little, is to prepare the way for that Artist Man whom you herald, who really dwells now in the physical man as a soul, and who is to come forth one day as an Animated Society. *True body* is the easiest way of altering mind, and I am deeply anxious to use it as such. Once dip into its Lake of Truths, I see no controversies ahead—nothing but reconciled parties and co-operating sinews. My work, however, will, I fear, be only suggestive; but even that will be something."

Of the need of some such work as he is doing, he wrote [1] :—

" When I look at the disconnection in science between man and his own body, I cease to wonder at the difficulty the great Emerson has in thinking of an incarnate God. Why, the philosophers have never yet got to think of man himself as incarnate. They admit either the flesh without the spirit, or the spirit without the flesh. The thought has yet to come which will combine the two. The present thought admits no incarnations whatever—not even

[1] Letter to Mr H. J. James, January 25, 1850.

F

those of lice and flies. It has two ends, ghosts and minerals, but no meaning, which are flesh."

" The Human Body " was published in May 1851, and dedicated to Mr James. It was published by subscription. The aim and method of the work appear in Wilkinson's " Proposal for Publishing." In it he says : " The human body, as an object of science, has hitherto been the property of one profession ; it has been studied only after death, when it is the reverse of human, to afford light to medicine, which takes no cognisance of it but when diseased. Death has slyly proffered *his* torch to the art of healing. A different study, not super-seding yet subjugating the former, is needed to connect the body with life, health, and business ; a study that brings the plain to illustrate the obscure, and the common to interpret the extraordinary. To further such a study is the object of the present work, in which we hope to show by examples that the anatomy of man is other than that of the dis-secting room, and that the knife is the feeblest although the first instrument for opening the mysteries of the human being."

A review of the book in the *New York Daily Tribune* says that it was probably the first attempt ever made, by a professional man, to connect the technical facts of anatomy and physiology with the truths of Revelation. " At all events it is the only one whose superb and lavish ability entitles it to an enduring mention. Ordinary men have no beliefs. They have only knowledge. . . . Yet this is precisely Dr Wilkinson's infatuation: he evidently believes what other people only remember. His memory is manifestly and wholly subservient to the highest intellectual uses. Nothing comes into it by the portals of sense which is not immediately divested of its dusty garments, and elevated into the chambers of the understanding, these to be associated with angelic company. He diligently gathers all that the best men and the most sacred books have said of God and man, but no symptoms of congestion appear, because the knowledge is instantly sublimated into belief, and thence descends in copious showers of influence upon all the fields of practical life. . . . Such exactly is Dr Wilkinson's force—the force of a man who is alive with glowing life from the centre of his intellect to the circumference. When such a man accordingly descends into the arena of the schools, we must not be surprised to see teaching assume a novel aspect, and old truths beam forth with quite original beauty. Those who wish an intellectual treat of the very highest description, a banquet in which every dish is made to yield the subtlest and most unexpected aromas, by a cooking the most expert and masterly ever practised, may safely be referred to the book whose name we have already cited."

" The Human Body " was widely read; indeed

it probably attained a more general repute than any other of Wilkinson's works. A second edition was published in 1860. Its original appearance was somewhat delayed by an interruption in the writing of it. Wilkinson received a commission for a translation. It appeared in 1852, " The Generative Organs considered Anatomically, Physically, and Philosophically. A posthumous work of Swedenborg, translated from the Latin."

At the end of 1850 the Wilkinsons moved again, to Sussex Lodge, St John's Wood. The house is nearly opposite to 4 Finchley Road, the home for nearly fifty years, where Dr Wilkinson died.

Prospects were beginning to look brighter. A letter to his father reports, in June 1851, " Our move to Sussex Lodge has been, so far, a very good thing for us ; my practice has greatly increased, and our connections are both extended and heightened. We have indeed constant struggles and wants, but we hope that the turn in our long lane of cares may be near at hand." It was so. The practice soon demanded and justified a carriage : and whatever care may have sat behind the rider was not due to want of a sufficient income.

A large and growing medical practice does not conduce to steady literary work; moreover, the study necessary to practise homœopathy is considerable and absorbing. But if for a time Wilkinson's pen was unproductive, he was using what leisure he had in preparing, perhaps unconsciously, for future literary work. The Norse languages had always attracted him. Perhaps it was an hereditary leaning, for his family is originally of Danish extraction. He gives a short account of his studies in the Preface to " Voluspa," writing in November 1897 : " At the end of a long life we yearn back and think biographically, and gentle readers will forgive a retrospect. So I tell them the story of my love of the far North. It is between forty and fifty years since I enjoyed my first acquaintance with the Eddaic Books. Tegner's ' Frithiof ' and his fine translation of ' Vafthrudhuismal ' were my lures into further reading. Through friends in Scandinavia the old Icelandic tongue came before me. The Lord's Prayer read in Icelandic made me say to myself, ' This is my language.' Rektor P. A. Siljeström, the schoolmaster of Sweden, and a master scholar of his country, a man of enduring scientific and liberal genius, read to me my first line of grammatical Old Norse. Ión A. Hjaltalin, my dear Icelander who found me in Reykiavik, became my teacher in London, and carried me through the Eddas.

Dr Siljeström was a great friend of Wilkinson's. When he left England for the United States, armed with an introduction to Mr James, he left his young wife at Hampstead with his English friends. Wilkinson " took the opportunity of her presence to learn a little Swedish." They had at this time a German guest also, Mr Neuberg, a friend of both Emerson and Carlyle. On June 24, 1837, Wilkinson wrote to Mr Emerson :—

" I have requested Mr Clapp to send you a copy of my work on ' The Human Body and its Connexion with Man,' just published; it is, I hope, in a double sense, my last book. I owe you a grudge for having in some part been a party to the book : for your good opinion of my former labours has had, I am sure, a certain egging effect upon me in this. Perhaps you will be so kind as to be a little sour and *un*satisfactory about the present, that you may contribute to warn me away from the strand of scribbling.

" My pursuit for relaxation this long time past has been Northern Literature and Languages, Swedish, Danish, and Icelandic; and the contents which these three bags carry are attractive to me at present. Mr Carlyle also is as deep as an old laundry-woman in these rich old clothes."

But his estimate of the contents of " those three bags " was much higher than Carlyle's.[1]

" I have lately been reading Carlyle's Essay on Odin in the ' Hero-Worship,' in pursuance of my present Scandinavian studies. What a useful affair it doubtless was, but what a poor thing it is ! He admits the inimitableness of this mythology,

[1] Letter to Mr H. I. James, January 25, 1850.

and yet humbly craves at last of his readers, to consent to admit that the authors of it were not downright fools! The prisoner at the bar has beaten the Greeks in majesty and depth, and all the thoughts of men in invention, pray you, Gentlemen of the jury, let the verdict be—' No jackass! ' . . . It is perfectly clear that Carlyle has no insight into the circumstances attending the production of these wonders of the Fore-time, or he would never have said that they were the first rude but powerful conceptions of the earliest gazers upon nature. We see here that he has been born in an atmosphere fetid with Scotch philosophers, which imposed upon him the belief in the original savagery of man."

His strong views on the receptivity of aboriginal man found full expression in " Revelation, Mythology, Correspondences " (1887) and in " The African and the True Christian Religion, his Magna Charta " (1892).

These studies were no temporary amusement. In 1855, Wilkinson writes to Mr James: " I am busy ; but still I find it necessary to interpolate my active life with some sort of recreation—with some fad entirely apart from physic. My Icelandic studies furnish me with this ; and I am going to send you, for my name-sake,[1] a translation of one of the Eddaic songs—' Hamar's Heimt '—Thor's

---

[1] One of Mr James' sons was christened " Garth Wilkinson" ; one of Wilkinson's daughters was " Mary James."

recovery of his hammer. Belonging to the childhood of our races, it will serve for our children,
as well as for our old gentlemen—that is to say,
both for the Boy and Old Henry. I have in my
vicinity a young sculptor of great promise, for whom
I have undertaken to make a few versions of these
wonderful songs, he intending to illustrate them;
and it is not impossible, if life and valour be given
for the next ten years, that I may even essay the
terribly ambitious work of a translation of the
'Elder Edda,' a work which, if well done, would
surprise literature; give Greece and Rome a thwack
unexpected, but wanted long; and shed a new
light upon the English language. It has for me also
an interest, in that it is the earliest, the most hoar
phenomenon, in the morning of our ages; while
Swedenborg, also of Scandinavia, is the latest hour
of the same day; and he who knows of both hears
deep calling unto deep."

For the main part, however, the practice of his
profession gives him enough to do. "When you pay
your promised visit," he writes to Mr James, in
May 1853, "I do not think that you will find me
altered to the extent that you have heard. It is
true I am now in a new pursuit which excludes all
old ones as active guests—though it leaves them
as subjects on which I rejoice to think that advancement is being made by others. Surely, my dear
Henry James, you would not cramp me by insisting

that I shall study, or without study swallow, your great batches of universals, when I solemnly tell you that they are out of my line. . . . Respect the blink-eyedness of the doctor who, in comparison with curing an old cough or a chronic gouty limb, thinks astronomy and theology to be for him of little moment, and of the cobbler who, for fear of diverting his skill from boot-soles, can't be got to look at the moon through the finest telescope that was ever framed. I am that Doctor and Cobbler, I never could do two things at once, and thence each pursuit, with me, implies the temporary incapacity for others."

There is something entertaining in Garth Wilkinson's plea to be treated mercifully as the possessor of " a one-storeyed intellect." In this very letter he shows the keenest interest in the spiritualism of that day. " The ferment all this produces shows that some great stirrer is a-troubling the waters; and, for my part, though I have not been near the spirits, I am quite convinced, and would avow it publicly, that the present movement is Providential in its best parts, in something more than the sense of permission : that it also belongs to the age; inasmuch as it is *cheap, easy, and ex-peditious Revelation*, or the *Spiritual World for the Million*, and that its lowness is the strong point and claim about it."

It appears that Wilkinson was firm so far as

abstaining from attendance at séances was concerned ;
but for years he lived in an atmosphere of " spiritualism." Those nearest to him were in association
with mediums and were moved to execute spirit-
drawings. His brother William was for many years
editor of the *Spiritual Magazine* ; and, in 1856,
Garth Wilkinson himself edited a number of the
Spiritual Herald. We shall soon reach his writing
of the " Improvisations from the Spirit." But he was
to escape from this " obsession " with a modified
opinion and a hearty dislike for the whole subject.
His final attitude is plain.[1] " I do not deny, but
prize, in their place, spontaneous motions of the
spiritual world upon and in the natural world.
If there be a spiritual world in proximity with
our world, such manifestations are, some of them,
according to order, and no one is chargeable with
them. On the other hand, solicited intercourse
with the spiritual world is, to me, a mistake, and,
with my convictions, it would be a sin to take part
in séances, or any other means, in such solicitation."
He refused to discuss either his own experiences
or the general subject, in conversation ; saying only
that he had gone into the matter extensively and
wished to say nothing about it.

In a letter to Mr James we get a glimpse of Wilkinson's political views at this time (July 1850). They

[1] Quoted without reference, in the *University Magazine,* June 1879,.
Art. " J. J. Garth Wilkinson."

were, like most of his views, highly eclectic. Sir Robert Peel had just died by accident, and the Duke of Wellington was not likely to be long spared to the country.

"No one so much represented England as he [Sir Robert Peel]. Even the *soubriquet* of ' Perfidious Albion ' was justified in its best sense in him. A man of continual expediency, he could never be bound to party save as the tool, and not the master of ever-shifting occasion. He got into parties, but his practical tendencies speedily won them and broke them up. And in this he was seconded by the ' Iron Duke,' who, apparently inflexible, is really flexible as a shirt of mail ; which, impenetrable from without, is yet jointed, and bends about to every requirement of the body politic. These two men have been the two great Revolutionists, *more Anglico*, and have succeeded in breaking up the old associations of parties to such an extent, that many years must elapse before a new party can be formed with any chance of coherence beyond the attainment of temporary objects. For to neither of them were political combinations regarded as hearty clubs with banners, watchwords, and ' no surrender ' tunes ; but simply as means, more or less useful, but subject to be superannuated and discarded as soon as ever the circumstances altered. They suffered much from the hot fragments of parties which they themselves had broken to atoms, but Providence had given them both prepared skins of courage and apathy; and they held out their ground until Sir Robert's death, as the two best defended and least offensive men in England. Their graves will be honoured by no majority or minority, but by the whole legislature and people of England."

This was the principle of Wilkinson's own method. His opinions were strong, and he supported them strongly; but he had kept means ever in their place, and was always ready to avail himself of new ones, but upon the means in use at any one time he concentrated his attention. It may have left him open to a charge of inconsistency at the hands of the superficial. That concerned him not at all. Nor was he able to conceive of anything except God, His laws and Word, as exempt from being some day "superannuated and discarded." He could calmly foresee a time when even Swedenborg's message would prove but provisional and preparatory for another. He was essentially an individualist and an eclectic. He was not *nullius addictus jurare in verba magistri*; rather, he was ready to hail any man as his master so long as, and only so long as, he could teach and help him forward in the matter in hand. The wise strong man has only one principle, the glory of his Maker; and his best way of furthering that is the education of his own character. Consistent in that, he can afford to appear inconsistent in all else.

As to politics, certainly, Wilkinson was to be found in various companies at various times. Mr Francis Newman, brother of the Cardinal, hailed him as a Republican in 1867 : he describes himself as a Conservative, in 1885. But his friend Mr Matheson defined his position more accurately, in 1888 : " I am Mathesonian in my political views, which I think have certain dissonances with Wilkinsonianism —that is to say, with a certain radically liberal conservatism."

In 1854, England had two great subjects to think about, the cholera and the Crimean War : the two insisted upon being considered together in the prevalence of cholera among our soldiers and sailors in the Crimea.

Wilkinson saw his opportunity and wrote, " War, Cholera, and the Ministry of Health, an Appeal to Sir Benjamin Hall and the British People." In the form of an open letter, it promulgates homœopathy as the medicine of the future. With its medical side we are not at present concerned ; but the reasoning power, the good temper, the wit and *aplomb* which Wilkinson showed in its pages brought him many readers. As a reviewer said, " If a man wants to see the faculty horsewhipped, or tossed in a blanket, or tried at the bar, or dressed in a cap and bells . . . we advise him to read Dr Wilkinson's ' Ministry of Health.' It is a most original piece of medical remonstrance, dressed up in festive style, like a Christmas box, or a New Year's Day gift. It contains both facts and fun and sharp surgical satire, with good humour combined." Statistics are relieved by sarcasm; pathos gives place to suggestions in practice: it even deals in prophecy which has since been fulfilled. For it foretells the medical woman. "Dr Blackwell[1] is already but one of a band of which Florence Nightingale is the English chief, and some of the best woman's blood in this country is speeding to the field of war to do woman's work as it has not been done before since the days of Jeanne d'Arc. I will not trust myself to think or to feel, while the Lord thus calls up His chosen into their long empty places, lest the brain should be drowned in the too great hour. Only I will say, it rejoices me that medicine (call it nursing if you please, but *it will not stop there*) is one thing which has unchained the feet of woman, and cast away her Chinese shoes." "The Ministry of Health" is a contribution to a controversy which now and again still comes before the public, and as such it is forgotten; but, as a long and sustained flight in true humour, it deserves readers and admirers at the present time.

In this book Wilkinson advocated registration of all who chose to practise physic. He returned more seriously to the same subject in an article which he wrote for the *British Journal of Homœo-*

---

[1] The first woman M.D. of the United States.

pathy, under the title of " Unlicensed Medicine " in 1855.

In 1856 he produced a curious pamphlet, " Painting *with both Hands*, or the Adoption of the Principle of the Stereoscope in Art, as a Means to Binocular Pictures," under the pseudonym John Love. The idea of the pamphlet was that " ambidextrous or two-handed painting will realize in art also binoculars or two-eyed pictures. . . . The suggestion of such a method, involving, as it does, a new and difficult education, would be monstrous if painting remained as it was ; but this, as I have said, is no longer the case ; for the stereoscope, by beating it on its own basis, has shown that it is not true to Nature, and moreover has demonstrated where the failing lies."

But the suggestion itself was based on a fallacy : Art does not aim to produce an image such as is seen through the stereoscope, but such as is seen through the eye ; and that, not in its entirety, but with selective power. " Painting with both Hands " contains, however, an amusing hit at Ruskin, who " hops along on one leg to criticism with a power and rapidity quite new ; and sometimes moves so fast that his hopping even mimics progress." The pamphlet did not found a new school of painting.

Wilkinson's next work was " Improvisations from the Spirit " (1857). An account of it is given in Gilchrist's " Life of William Blake " (vol. i. p. 382).

" A very singular example of the closest and most absolute resemblance to Blake's poetry may be met with (if only one *could* meet with it) in a phantasmal sort of little book, published, or perhaps not published, but only printed, some years since, and entitled ' Improvisations of (*sic*) the Spirit.' It bears no author's name, but was written by Dr J. J. Garth Wilkinson, the highly gifted Editor of Swedenborg's writings, and author of a Life of him, to whom we owe a reprint of the poems in Blake's ' Songs of Innocence and Experience.' These improvisations profess to be written under precisely the same kind of spiritual guidance, amounting to abnegation of personal effort in the writer, which Blake supposed to have presided over the production of his ' Jerusalem,' etc. The little book has passed into the general (and, in all other cases, richly deserved) limbo of the modern ' Spiritualistic ' muse. It is a very thick little book, however unsubstantial its origin ; and contains, amid much that is disjointed or hopelessly obscure (but then, why be the polisher of poems for which a ghost, and not even your own ghost, is alone responsible ?), many passages, and indeed whole compositions of a remote and charming beauty, or sometimes of a grotesque, figurative relation of things of another sphere, which are startlingly akin to Blake's writings—could pass, in fact, for no one's but his. Professing, as they do, the same new kind of authorship, they might afford plenty of material for comparison and bewildered speculation, if such were in any request."

Wilkinson's own account of the genesis of this book is as follows (quoted, without reference, in *The University Magazine*, June 1879):

" A theme is chosen and written down. So soon as this is done, the first impression upon the mind which succeeds the act of writing the title, is the beginning of the evolution of that theme, no matter how strange or alien the word or phrase may seem. . . . An act of faith is signalized in accepting the first mental movement, the first word that comes as the response to the mind's desire for the unfoldment of the subject. . . . Reason and will are not primary powers in this process, but secondary, not direct, but regulative; and imagination, instead of conceiving and constructing, only supplies words and phrases piece-meal, or however much it receives; it is as a disc on which the subject is projected, not as an active concipient organ."

It must be remembered, firstly, that Wilkinson showed some power of versifying, when a boy at school, and that he was then a greedy reader of poetry; secondly, that Blake was the only poet whom (so far as we know) he had studied systematically and exhaustively since that time. The only other contribution towards judgment which shall be added here is that no doubt can exist concerning Wilkinson's serious simplicity in his account of the

G

" influx " to which he considered himself subject. With these helps the reader must judge of the matter for himself.

Two specimens of these " Improvisations " may, however, be welcome, since the book which contains them is practically unobtainable.

Shall my Poet cup
Now be driéd up?
Yes: it shall dry up now, to ope again:
And then it shall disclose a deeper vein,
And more abundant waters, when thy health
And Faith and Hope and Good are greater Wealth
Of Poet-Power within thee : then thy heart
Shall be more full of courage, and have part
In fountains not so easily exhaust.
At present thou art Vanity's Holocaust,
And greatly burnt up by her love of Beauty,
For sake of Beauty's show—so, do thy Duty:
And song shall come in bright Attendances:
And specially when upon thy knees,
Thou dost invite the Muse Celestial down.
At other times she does but sit and frown,
While lower spirits, not songful, leering sprites,
Usurp her harp-strings, and put out her lights.
Heaven, the Heart's Heaven, and Home, the land of God,
Is the Parnassus on whose mystic sod
The Muses build their real mansion.   Life
Is the great field whereon the heavenly Strife
And heavenly harmony of Song do enter,
And where in unison of Love they centre.
Make thy Home Heaven, then, and then Poesy
Married to Christ, love shall well visit thee.
Farewell till then: for until then we flee.
Cowley and Herbert's sphere
Are no longer here.

I asked, Can I write Song this morning ?

Yes, you can, with power and sweetness too. .
Your Muse is here: you nothing have to do,
But to sit by, while she indites the Song:
Her brightness flows around you, and ere long,
You will so recognize her friendly hand,
That naught shall intervene to countermand
God's will with you, that you be instrument,
To work out His most holy high intent
Of pouring Truth, apart from mortal pride,
Upon all men who willingly abide,
In Truth's and Beauty's way: so take your pen,
Be a good boy; and down to earth again
Shall step sweet Spirit-Melodies, more rare
Than ever yet have thrilled thy native air.

The book has always had admirers and adherents, and Wilkinson was frequently importuned for copies. Dr Westland Marston, acknowledging a presentation copy, says :—" I find matter of deep psychological interest. I value it for its spirit which seems to me an utterance of the law or essence of which objects are exponents ; although the *forms* are occasionally perplexed. There are perpetual glints of spiritual life and revelations which could not be got at by any process of straining, though the two sets of images often run the one into the other. . . . Clearly the book, proceeding from the initial force of the mind, rather than from the representative faculties, will only be patent to the initial mind—to the initiated : but by such it will be deeply valued." Another

correspondent, writing as late as 1871, says :—" You
have assuredly long ago heard from far worthier
lips the just recognition of their value ; but I cannot
forbear expressing to you my deep sense of the
mingled charm of strong simplicity and mystic
splendour that characterize so many of them."
But " the initiated " are few, and Mr Gilchrist's
dictum, that the book has passed into the limbo of
the modern " spiritualist " muse, must be accepted.
Still, two poems, those upon " Turner " and " The
Diamond " appear in the little known authology
of verse which Mr Emerson issued under the title
" Parnassus."

This year, 1857, saw a very different production
of Wilkinson's pen—a pamphlet upon " The Use
of Glanderine and Farcine in the treatment of
Pulmonary and other Diseases " which introduced
two new *nosodes* to medical practice. Another
pamphlet, embracing the two influences which were
then potent upon him, was " The Homeopathic
principle applied to Insanity, a proposal to treat
Insanity by Spiritualism."

There follow several years in which Wilkinson
published little.   In 1858 he took his son James, then
a boy of fourteen, with him for a tour in Norway and
Sweden, at that time regarded as a piece of serious
travel.   It is not necessary to follow them through
the experiences of a holiday now sufficiently usual ;
but one extract may be quoted from his letters as

evidence of his delight and appreciation of what he saw.[1]

" I am almost stunned by the magnificence and fearful beauty of Nature in these Norse wildernesses of mountains. Lake upon lake,. waterfall upon waterfall, mountains barren as stones, mountains clad with heather, with fir trees, with superb various forests, emerald pictures of farms hung up here and . there in the halls of the giants : you have no conception of it. Tell our friend Mr Shrubsole that here are Rockeries by the thousand miles together. . . . The might of water here, doubling and embracing all the great creations, which see themselves like thoughts within it, is something unparalleled to my mind. Only just now we have visited near our Hotel, a foss or waterfall, the descent of a great river through deep stony gorges into the subjacent lake, which at first took away my powers of appreciation. It is the realm of the Poetry of the Giants. . . . Jamie drives himself like a Norwegian."

During this year Garth Wilkinson's eldest daughter, Emma, was betrothed to Lieut. Hermann Pertz, son of G. H. Pertz.[2]

The marriage was a happy one to all concerned and gave great interest in all German matters to the family. The two daughters of this union were,

---

[1] Letter to his wife, August 7, 1858.

[2] Editor of "Monumenta Germaniæ Historica," and author of " Stein's Leben."

after the death of their parents, to supply bright and loving company to Garth Wilkinson in his old age.

Spiritualism contributed a strange acquaintance in Thomas Lake Harris. Writing to a follower of Harris,[1] Wilkinson says :—

" Mr and Mrs Harris stayed with me in this house for some weeks when they first visited London. I have many memories of them both. Afterwards they lodged in Queen's Terrace, close to this, during the whole time of his delivery of his sermons in Wigmore Street, in what is now Steinway Hall. In that Hall I also heard both Carlyle and Emerson lecture. There is a poem in Regina—addressed to my late daughter, Emma Marsh Pertz.

" When Harris visited London some years after, he passed me by, and was with the Oliphants and others. It was a proof of his spiritual judgment. for in the meantime I had departed from anything like pupilage to his genius, and gradually left Spiritualism on any other than the lines of the New Religion commissioned through Swedenborg. I do not, however, close myself against any future dispensation. But I cannot see that T. L. Harris has continued the Revelation of the Divine Sense of the Word, though he has broken ground in social and practical life : perhaps deep ground."

Lawrence Oliphant was also a friend of this period. " To-day I have a present of West India Jams from

---

[1] Letter to Mr J. Thomson, September 1, 1893.

Mrs Bennett, Mr Oliphant's friend," wrote Wilkinson in 1865. " He wants to go to Mr Harris in America. *Their difficulty seems coming.*" There was perhaps more than " spiritual judgment " in Harris' avoidance of his former host; for when Oliphant pressed Wilkinson for an introduction to Harris, Wilkinson declined it, with the expressed opinion that the acquaintance was not for Oliphant's good. It had been well for the latter if he had accepted his friend's opinion. But he went to Queen's Terrace, walked outside Harris' lodgings for some time in doubt, and finally introduced himself to " the Prophet," with results which will be remembered by all who have read his biography.

The last contemporary mention of Harris, in the same year, reads, " Harris is starting a Bank, of which he is President." Wilkinson does not appear to have been a depositor.

In the same letter, he mentions, " The day before yesterday I had a long talk with Mr and Mrs G. H. Lewes. *Romola* was very nice, and looked particularly well."

Among the letters of 1859 is one from Lola Montez, who seeks Garth Wilkinson's acquaintance on account of his position in the New Church, his authorship of the " Improvisations," and his connection with T. L. Harris.

These years were full of professional work, and that is very probably the reason why they have left few

traces of other interests.   Charles Lamb said that
the true works of Elia were to be found in the ledgers
of India House.   The writings of Garth Wilkinson
between 1857 and 1880 must, in general, be sought
in his Case Books.   During this time he established
a consulting room at 76 Wimpole Street and moved
house to 4 Finchley Road.   In 1865 he delivered
a discourse upon " Our Social Health " before
The Ladies' Sanitary Association, which was afterwards published, and ran through two editions:
it set forth righteousness, both public and private,
as an essential to social well-being.   His holidays
bulk largely in his correspondence, perhaps because
he found more time for writing then than during
the working months.   These holidays were varied
and extensive.

In 1859, starting late in consequence of his
daughter's wedding, Wilkinson went South, to Algiers,
via Marseilles, then home by Arles, Nismes and Lyons.
He wrote, among others, a lively letter to his son.

" I arrived just before the Annual Arab Races,
which the French Government has instituted, by
premiums, to improve the breed of Arab Horses.
The town was full of Arab cavaliers, from all parts,
even to the great desert: all Tribes, such figures
as you have seen in books, at full gallop, with lance
and matchlock.   From 5 to 6 thousand men were
encamped on Mustapha Superieure, a place above
the town, where also we saw troops of camels.

In the race, 7 Arabs started every 5 minutes, for four hours, and the victor, the moment his steed came in, leapt down, and was paid his premium. It was a strange sight, to see these wild people, with their rude turbans and long garments of flannel, with naked legs, flying past in fierce competition on their Arab horses. Then the sides of the course were occupied also by the picturesque chivalry of the Atlas. Besides these, there were the dapper French Officers and multitudes of Moors, Jews, Negros; a mixture of many nations. One or two Arabs were killed in the rush; one very near me. The French have an ambulance bed on the course ready to receive them; and, one moment in all the fire of rivalry, the next they are being walked off in their coffins. Their Arab *frères* take no notice and a few deaths are considered a matter of course."

The sunshine, the mixture of races, and the fruit, of which he gives a picturesque catalogue, appear to have most impressed him.

In 1860, there was another wedding in the family, his second daughter marrying Mr B. St John Matthews (afterwards Attwood-Matthews) of Pontrilas Court, Herefordshire. The holiday of this year took him to Paris, Brussels and Malines. Paris, not being in revolution, did not please him so much as it had done in 1848.

In 1861 he took an autumn trip to Spain with his friend Mr Decimus Hand, meeting on board ship with General Outram, "who in these his last days is quite a picture and a study to me. He talks very unreservedly of his past life." The route was by Gibraltar, Cadiz, Xeres (where he "tasted sherry at the fountain head"), Seville, Cordova and Granada with the Alhambra. The Cathedral of Seville greatly impressed him. "At 9 this morning we went into the Cathedral, which made me literally heave with emotion. Hands said, "I say, Wilkinson, doesn't this knock one to pieces?" To say that it beggars and eclipses all the ecclesiastical edifices I have seen conveys no idea of what I felt. Art in the grandest shape yet realized, one feels that it is also Nature, and that rock and mountain would own it as a sister. It is so stupendous in size and weight, that Antwerp or Notre Dame dwindles before its columns. And the lights that play within it, by their intensity of colour, give a kind of awful finish, though ever shifting, to the interior. We also ascended the Moorish Tower, 340 feet, the easiest ascent I ever made, and saw the view of Seville, of a village on the hill where Cortez lived, the Bull Ring, the Guadalquiver, etc. But coming back to the Cathedral, the view looked small, to the surprizing inside."

Characteristic of the man was his intense love of light and of trees. He seldom visited a place without recording some enjoyment gained from one or both of them. It will be remembered that in his autobiographical fragment he mentions the joy which he felt as a boy on a certain "picnic of picnics" on meeting with "junipers and other plants of such regions, which were as parts of a new world to him." Writing to his youngest daughter, on this Spanish journey, he heads his letter :

"ALHAMBRA !! *September* 25, 1861 :—

"The above will speak volumes. I am not writing *within* the precincts of the Alhambra! I shall not waste words with descriptions : but only say that all words fail to convey an idea of this ruin with its surroundings. It and Granada are the *Arabian Nights* made into a palace and city. You cannot see the El Hamar (Alhambra) without the sun-green gardens, of Orange, Pomegranate, Vine, Fig, and all other most blooming and aromatic creatures : nor it, or these, without the sun-blue sky, paved as it is here with its own light, reflected up in one great column from mountain and plain, as far as the eye can reach. In all the sight there is a glow, as though we were feeling in the day the immediate pulsation of the sun. And the men and women one sees, as well as the piled fruits, seem as if they were the result and natural jewel of all these influences.

"I speak only on the picturesque side, and attempt to throw you a copper, representing the Imperial Coinage of the beauty of this old Moorish place, as it is embalmed in the true beauty of God's great Nature."

The possessor, or possessed, of such enthusiasm did well to travel; but he had an eye quick to see the humbler beauties of the garden. Writing to the same daughter (Mrs Claughton Mathews) in 1898, he says :—

"It seems absurd to talk to you, any of you, about greenwoods; either in Brockenhurst or Sevenoaks. But the happiness of a patch of blue precocious squills, and of daffodils and primroses and oxlips fills the conceit until I think of my little flower-beds as country scenery, embosomed now also in horse-chestnut trees great and small, revelling in live bold buds, the promise of Spring."

The last time I saw him, only a few weeks before his death, when his walks were confined to the little London garden behind his home, Garth Wilkinson showed me, with affectionate satisfaction, some of his garden treasures, reminiscent of sunny days of travel; a chestnut grown from a nut which he had picked up at Cordova, *Hydrastis Canadensis* brought from the States, *Phytolacca* sent to him by a friend in New Zealand. His mind's eye could still reconstruct the scenes where these things had flourished at their best, and he was warmed and lighted up by memory.

In 1863 his holiday took him no farther than Scotland and the English Lakes; and in 1864 he

paid a delightful visit to his daughter, Mrs Pertz,
and his infant grandchildren, at Salzburg; seeing
Nuremburg, Innsbruck and Vienna, in company with
Captain Pertz.

1866 took him to Iceland, which appealed to him
so keenly that he repeated the journey in 1868.
Journals of both visits are full of keen observation
and great enjoyment. Icelandic travel in those
days was regarded as distinctly adventurous, and
there was a good deal of roughness and discomfort
in the experience : but it was salutary. " All our
party," he wrote, " seems better than usual ; and
for my part I cannot doubt that it is more feasible
for me to be here on this rough platform of experience,
than to be enjoying the luxuries of good hotels in
pleasant places on the Continent. I feel strengthen-
ing for my dear work at home." The greatest danger
that he escaped was from an unexpected eruption
of the Great Geyser while he was bathing in a warm
pool. Tons of boiling water fell on the place he had
occupied but a moment before.

Here, as elsewhere, he made friends. Mr Ion
a Hyaltalin helped him much, as we have seen,
in his study of the language. He came to England
later, became Librarian of the Advocates' Library
in Edinburgh, returned home, and is now head of
a College in Mödruvellir. The friendship was close
and life-long.

The holiday of 1869 realized the hopes of many

years. It took the form of a rush through part
of the United States. He was away from home
only five weeks. The poet, Longfellow, and his
family, were on board the steamer on the outward
journey, and with them Wilkinson foregathered.
He saw New York, Albany, Niagara, Montreal,
Quebec, Lake Champlain, Lake George, Boston and
Cambridge. Here he was fraternally received by
Mr James, and renewed the unbroken friendship
of old times. Wilkinson found his god-son an
ex-captain and farmer on a large scale, who, having
fought and bled in command of a negro Regiment,
can hope no better for the coloured brother than that
he may die out. From Mr James' house Wilkinson
visited Longfellow, with whom he found Charles
Sumner, Chairman of the Committee for Foreign
Affairs in the Senate, and notorious at this time
for his fierceness over the Alabama Claims. Though
he was conciliatory and " claimed " to be a reader
of Wilkinson's works, on the recommendation of
Emerson, the conversation ended in an outspoken
argument. Old patients, old literary colleagues, new
friends who were old readers, fell in Wilkinson's way
at every turn : he found himself famous in the States,
his name a pass-word. It is not to be wondered at
that he enjoyed his hurried holiday.

On his return home, he wrote in his travelling
journal a reply to the constant question which had
greeted him. " What do you think of our country ? "

" Sitting at home here, Jonathan, Brother and dear Boy, I like what I have seen of it very extremely ; and even feel that I fantastically regret having spent holidays in France, Germany, Switzerland and other old and irrelevant places, when I might earlier have grasped your singular and ever-grasping fingers.

" I was fourteen days and some hours there, and felt the touch of a new life, a new vitality, a new velocity in everybody. I was impressed spiritually with the fact of a new Mission in Humanity, which America is carrying out : a mission the basis and nutriment of which is Making Money and Getting on ; not the All-mighty Dollar, but the indefinitely plentiful Dollar as a Divine Need for men to execute their Mission. I was impressed with the Divine Value of Money as distinctively opposed to the Aristocratic and Avaricious value of it, with the fact that every man is determined to make it by some services, to have it and to spend it. A new consciousness of the worth of Life in Cash ; a consciousness for want of which the operatives of Europe, save in the Trades Unions, are rotting.

" 2. I was impressed with the fact that the American People is Providentially hurled over the steeps and difficulties of their Continent, fearless and therefore free, to lay hold of it hour by hour, and cover it with roads and cities ; and to show how rapid an Architect Freedom is, in a new world all his own. And that this period of New Building of all kinds is not the making of a new Country, but of a Cosmopolitan Place, veritably a New World; which will destroy Countries and institute the World. That all lands will open into it, by henceforth vast migrations; and that by example, influence and polity it will educate, flow into and impress all countries, and be the crowning piece in the material life of the Nations, and that God is palpably with America all the time, and that it is Newly His, and will kneel more reverently to Him than any other World of Peoples.

And that the Vices and Corruptions of America are of the greatest, but do not hinder her first mighty Work; but will be burnt up as dried tares when the day of her purgation comes. And that now they are spiritually less deadly, though more odorously offensive, than the perfumed and fine-skinned Vices of European States."

Wilkinson, on his return, was strongly impressed with the necessity for the repeal of the Contagious Diseases (Women) Act. Mrs Josephine Butler and Mr F. W. Newman, the Cardinal's brother, were his friends, and it was not long before he took his place by their side. The periodical inspection of prostitutes in naval and military towns was a matter which made him white with anger and indignation. He wrote an open letter of sixteen pages to the Home Secretary, Mr Bruce, in which he stated his views with every plain statement of medical circumstance which could make the administration of the Act horrible and loathsome in the minds of his readers. Hating the subject, hating to write of it, he did so, once and for all, that others might hate it as he did. "The Forcible Introspection of Women for the Army and Navy by the Oligarchy considered physically" is painful reading. Whatever views may be held upon the subject, it is now unnecessary that this little pamphlet should be read. In a tract entitled "A Free State and Free Medicine," further advocating the dischartering of his profession, Wilkinson dealt also with this subject. At the same time we find him strongly supporting the Married Woman's Property Bill, in a letter to Mrs Jacob Bright.

Those of us who are old enough remember the intense excitement in England concerning the Franco-Prussian War, how general sympathy was first opposed to France and came round to her in her *débâcle*. It was sure to be otherwise in Wilkinson's household, who had a son-in-law fighting in the Prussian Engineers. As usual, Wilkinson "did not mince matters." On August 12, 1870 he wrote to his wife. "The evil of the day is that they (the Prussians) have been wantonly assaulted and invaded by 'Diaboleon,' and that they are obliged to resist to the death, and to put an end to the state of things which 'Diaboleon' represents. And they are doing it with a speed and certainty

H

which seems favoured of Heaven. Never before
has there been a more sublime spectacle of a great
Nation moving without a break from home into
battle, against a mere standing army of bandits
and cut-throats led by a murderous Devil. The
result will show that a standing Army has no chance
against an embattled people. . . . ' Diaboleon '
said well that ' he went to increase Liberty and
Civilization.' He did. A deeper Diaboleon, whose
fool he is, sent him forth, and in the destruction
of Self and Host, Liberty and Civilization will breathe
afresh, even for poor, but soon emancipated, France."

Many prayers were sent up for the safety of
Hermann Pertz who saw much service, was the
first Officer to enter Metz, received the Iron Cross
at Versailles and returned safely to his family, amidst
a chorus of thanksgiving.

Wilkinson had long foreseen German Unity.
Writing to his daughter Mrs Pertz in 1866 during
" The Seven Weeks' War," he said :—" I am deeply
interested in all you tell me of dear Hermann, for
whose preservation I am thankful to God ; and also
in the European conflict. If Prussia were a liberal
power, she might unite Germany into one nationality.
. . . At present, all she can do is to overrun alien
Germany ; but she will be unable to hold whatever
she cannot Prussianize ; for Prussianization appears
to be the height and depth and breadth of her aim,
and a very poor aim it is to justify the loss of so

many lives. But God may engraft His own ends upon the small aims of Kings and Ministers, and force the little fellows to carry them out; as he engrafted Total Emancipation upon the pettifogging Aims of the United States, and they had to fight till it was gained."

In October 1870, Wilkinson joined Mrs Pertz in Berlin. Writing to his wife the day after his arrival, he says. " Thank God, I am safe and well in this comfortable Hotel, and have just break-fasted in my bedroom, with our own Emma, and the boys beside me. They were here by 9 in the morning to see Grossvater in bed, in which they succeeded. . . . There are no regiments visible on the road, and almost no young men; this nation is evidently in a great crisis. Every-one seems quiet and composed; no boasting. The wounded in every train; we had three in my carriage. . . . France has no great cause to band her against the great cause that they (the Germans) have, the Unity of a Great German Fatherland. . . . She has caught her Conqueror. *His* doom is to conquer and to chain her for a time. No light doom either." On October 22, he writes, " At 10 to-day we went to the Wounded, with 144 jackets, socks and comforters, besides cigars. We were through at 1. Mrs Pertz [1] (senior) went with us, and we met at the hospital barracks the Countess

---

[1] *Née* Horner, wife of G. H. Pertz.

Stein, who accompanied us, also with stores. She spoke in such splendid terms of Emma and all she did at Strassburg; of her courage and rapidity. You should see Emma among the flocks of soldiers; she quite towers, and addresses them in the easiest way; and evidently loves service among them, touched, no doubt, continually by her absent Hermann. I am astonished at her, for she so thoroughly heads and leads the relieving party. We gave to Germans and French; and I had pleasant chats with the latter. You have only to see the whole stalwart faces of the Germans, their build, and contrast with the French, to know that that set of Germans once awakened and once victorious, the French would have no chance in the greater game of War.''

This year saw the beginning of Wilkinson's crusade against compulsory vaccination. His labours in this regard occupied his pen and his leisure extensively for some eight or nine years. It is a matter which will be best considered in a separate chapter.

In 1871, Mary James, Wilkinson's youngest daughter, was married to Mr Francis Claughton Mathews. It was a union which began a close and affectionate friendship, lasting through the remainder of Wilkinson's life. The marriage of his children gave Wilkinson ties near home and contributed with his age (for he was now nearing his sixtieth birthday), to diminish his zest for distant and rapid holiday excursions. Indeed we may regard his holidays of this and the next year as marking the end of such travel, in an orgy of two consecutive trips to Norway. His journal of the first of these journeys abounds in descriptions of scenery by land and sea and pleasantly reflects the sunshine flecked with sea-birds. " I have a most delightful Captain," he writes to his wife, " who quite pets me; the constant change of people at the *Stationer*; the putting off of the boats; and the men and women who come on board, is a pleasant study for a holiday time. And then, sea, sky, mountains, all clear and sweet, for hundreds and thousands of miles. . . . I am on deck nearly all day; enjoying the warm fresh air, and conversing about with the passengers." His son was contemplating the construction of a railway line from Sundsvall to Trondhjem, and he was busy in collecting information: the Swedes were opposed to it, as likely to exhalt Trondhjem at the expense of Stockholm. " They say the Swedish Government hinders it. Probably this is a Norwegian mistake. But, from what I hear, I cannot but think that the Railway will be made." James Wilkinson also engineered the Luleå line, the first and only railway which crosses the Arctic circle.

Wilkinson's speculative imagination was still active, " Loud carousing in the Cabin," he reported

on one of the outward journeys, " Constant Toasts "
—" Skal "—for " lyckliga neise." " What can toasts
mean ?   They seem generally to be convivial prayers,
with the Principal Character left out. . . . As I
noticed of the clouds in going to Iceland, so here, not
only of the clouds, but of the rocks and mountains,
I see that animal and human forms are constantly
suggested.   Men's faces on the fell-tops, tortoises,
elephants, all huge mammals, seem impacted, and
struggling in bonds of stone here.   All folks notice
it.   Is there not a *nisus animalis* and *nisus humanus*
really signified, a spiritual moulding inevitable,
in these things called freaks of Nature, and creatures
of the imagination ?   I believe it, and that no Alp
can be upheaved, and no rock settle, without feeling
that inner force of God by which all nature tends to
higher forms and to man.   The more plastic the
sphere, the more representative ;   so that cloudland
shows it most dramatically.   But granite obeys
also, and is from within, as well as from without,
a creature of the Divine and Human Imagination."

In a long-delayed letter to Mrs Pertz, at about
this time, Wilkinson bewails his inability to do more
than meet the absolute daily necessities of correspondence.   His practice now was very large and he
had frequently to visit patients at considerable
distances — such as Eastbourne, Oswestry and
Leamington.   He found his relaxation chiefly in
reading ;   the Norse studies were pursued, and he

began a course of the Latin Classics which he followed
with occasional interruptions to the end of his life.
Virgil, especially the sixth Æneid, was a favourite
of his; and he was pleased to meet anyone who
would discuss Lucretius with him. Plautus and
Terence amused him greatly. He was less addicted
to Greek. His holidays were now spent chiefly in
visiting his married daughters in Herefordshire and
in Kent. In 1875, however, he spent a few weeks
in Guernsey and enjoyed it; but he found an air
of retired gentility about the island which would
not long have contented him. In 1879, he paid
his last visit to Major and Mrs Pertz, at the Althof
Loetzen in East Prussia, where the Major was Com-
mandant of a small fortress. This Wilkinson duly
inspected, but it is characteristic of him that after
noting that " it is a great order " he proceeds to
mention the presence of wildflowers and the dis-
turbance of a hare from her form on one of the
slopes. The Major's overgrown garden and its cure
by clearances and pruning gave him great joy.
Major Pertz retired soon after this visit and found
occupation on the newly constructed Lynn and
Fakenham Railway, the work of James Wilkinson
junior. But he did not long survive his retirement
and died at Holt in Norfolk. It was the first entry
of death into Wilkinson's immediate family circle,
and he was deeply touched. Hermann Pertz
was a dear friend as well as the husband of a

loved and loving daughter for more than twenty years.

In 1882 Wilkinson translated from the Swedish a tract by his friend Rektor Siljeström upon the Vaccination question, entitled " A momentous Education question for the consideration of Parents and others who desire the well-being of the Rising Generation." A second edition was called for in the following year. He also wrote a little account of " Swedenborg's Doctrines and the Translation of his Works," a contribution to a series of New Church Tracts. It was a subject upon which no living man could speak with greater authority. " As one who has had some experience in translating Swedenborg," he says, " I can aver that at first for a length of time I had the feeling that it would be easy and right to popularize him somewhat, and to melt down his *Proprium* and his *Scientifics*, his *Goods*, *Truths* and *Uses* and many other of his terms. I tried my hand and failed. I found that none but Ulysses can bend the bow of Ulysses : that Swedenborg in Latin must be Swedenborg in English ; and so at last I came close to his terms, and, as far as I could get, got into their marrow ; and then I did not want to melt them down, but felt sure then, as I feel now, that they are a genuine coinage which the reader when he learns it, will never wish to see defaced in any least lineament, lest a value which is priceless be lost or altered thereby.

I learned, in short, that the terms are from the rational mint of the New Dispensation, and that it is not lawful to break or vary the coins of that Kingdom into other forms."

If the reader will be at the pains to compare a passage of the original Swedenborgian Latin with Wilkinson's translation he will see how modest is the claim which the translator sets forward for his work. He will be inclined to claim more for him; and to say that Wilkinson mastered the use of Elizabethan prose for this purpose. The English of the translations is the English of the Authorized Version of the Scriptures, the comprehensive and comprehensible English of Cranmer's Collects in the Book of Common Prayer.

In 1883, Wilkinson edited for his friend the Reverend J. le G. Brereton, a paper entitled *One Teacher: one Law* which demonstrated "the essential oneness of the Old and the New Testaments." In the same year he brought out, on his own account, a *brochure* on "Pasteur and Jenner" in which he bound Vivisection and Vaccination together for the purpose of gibbeting them the more effectually. He also write a tractate on "The Treatment of Small-pox by Hydrastis Canadenses and Veratrun vivide" and followed it in 1884 by another one, "Vaccination as a source of Small-pox."

1885 was a productive year in literary output; nor did the quality of the work show any degeneration.

A translation of Swedenborg's "*Sapientia Angelica de Divino Amore*" appeared. It consists of fifteen pages of introduction and 344 pages of text. The last of Wilkinson's translations from his master's works, it shows his matured skill as well as his vigour and perseverance. "The Greater Origins and Issues of Life and Death" followed. "This," as the preface explains, " was commenced in order to furnish to the public mind the Author's testimony and convictions concerning what is called Vivisection. . . . The determination of his heart and intellect against it has grown with his growth, strengthened with his strength. He has written upon it from time to time. And now, when a great public opinion is rising by his side, he had been compelled to put forth all his strength as one combatant in the cause of common humanity and common science."

" Medical Specialism " was originally an article contributed to the *Homœopathic World*, which was reprinted. It deals with a favourite subject of its author's—the specializing of and in the Practice of Medicine.

In a letter to his daughter Mrs Frank Mathews, he gives the following account of his feelings and doings at this time :—

" As I get older, care settles down more heavily ; but I have not yet discovered whether it is that there is more real care, or that I make the matter more onerous. Probably the latter. However, I am truly glad that this year I have been allowed to complete two Books, and to have them in my past. My translation of Swedenborg's 'Divine Love and Wisdom' is the most important literary work of my life; I have been through it in various editions some six times, and have now done my best with it. You will be glad to hear that my labours are hailed and appreciated warmly both in this country and in America; and that my own Book is selling as well as I can expect on both sides of the Atlantic. There is a good demand for it in Canada. If bodily health continues, there are still other subjects on which I should wish to speak; especially theological-political, on the rule of a true Church in and over Democracy. . . . But whether I am strong enough to enter this field, time and health will show. I like to tell you these things; for they are the only intimate part of me, and I wish you to participate in them.

"Dear Mamma and I are very happy together, especially in being at one in all our best hopes and beliefs; and in waiting with a patience which is a new and good fruit of years. In the midst of all our many anxieties for all our dear families, she is always buoyant at the end, and submissive to the Will, which is above our dictation. She is reconcilable to events by a Power above herself."

The "waiting with patience" for one of the partners was not to be long, for in March 1886, came the great sorrow of Wilkinson's life, the sorrow which one of every pair of lovers must expect. The loving and comprehending companion of forty-six years of happy wedded life had latterly been failing in health, and was taken from him. Neither religion nor philosophy can obviate the impact of such a blow at first; while self is self, the removal of so much must shock what of us is not stunned. In this way Garth Wilkinson suffered; but he knew well how near is the spirit world, how continuous with that which is ours; and he emerged, dismayed but not perplexed, from the first inevitable selfishness of grief. It was from the depth of experience and conviction that he wrote to the widow of a dear and recently lost friend. " You have both of you changed worlds; he is in sight of his Home, perhaps in it : you are in the Faith and Good of it, as you were not when he was here. It is sure that where conjugal love exists, the death of either mate increases and elevates the union as no other happening can."

Wilkinson was now seventy-three; he had not lost heart, but he was weary and had lost his chief earthly support. He had already given up his consulting room in Wimpole Street, and henceforth he retired, so far as he was allowed to do so, from the practice of his profession. There were old and loved patients whom he could not abandon; these he still received at his house and visited when necessary; but he would not add to their number.

He was far from idle, however. His interest in life and in all questions of the day remained keen to the last. If his aim had been to prolong his life—and he once told Crabbe Robinson that he wished to see his century, " to see the world flower open and the great things that will be, and to help,"—he could not have acted more wisely, for interest is the great physical spring of life. He was still conscious of a message to be delivered, he wished to reinforce work he had done in the past. His toleration became more wide, his judgments more gentle, his affections more general. He voluntarily and consciously entered into old age, but it was an old age of mental beauty, of good humours, of kindliness and wisdom : qualities which not only endeared him to old friends, but which also brought him new ones, and that not seldom among the young. People sought him out and asked leave to visit him ; they came with questions on all sorts of subjects and went away with information gathered from wide reading and wider observation. Seldom can there have been a man who was less, in the unpleasant American phrase, " a back number." He was in touch with the thinking and working men in all his favoured subjects, and, if they came to him for advice or information, he usually drew something from them for his own mental store.

At this time he was good to see. Above six feet in height and but little bowed by time ; inclined

to stoutness but far from unwieldiness; bearded
almost to the waist, the hair grizzled but still showing some of its original brown; but slightly bald
over a high-domed forehead; thick and rough of
eyebrow over keen blue eyes which flashed under
his gold-rimmed spectacles; handsome and tidy in
his dress, he was a fine specimen of a cultured and
kindly gentleman. His voice was charming, strong,
vigorous and deep as the thought behind it; prone
to hearty laughter, but not rarely a little broken
by anything of grandeur and pathos which had
touched him. It was a voice which comes back to
those who knew him as they read his books or recall
his talk. His enunciation was remarkably clear,
without any trace of precision, as his conversation
was full of learning without pedantry. Sitting by
his dwarf revolving bookcase, on which rested his
snuff box and a pile of books in many languages
and on many subjects, he made a picture which
never rises in the memory of his friends without
bringing pleasure and thankfulness with it.

In 1887 Wilkinson brought out " Revelation,
Mythology, Correspondences," a work in which he
set himself to show that Revelation was not confined
to the Jewish and Christian Churches, but that the
ancient mythologies, read by the light of correspondences, was full of Divine teaching; that there
was, in fact, a golden primæval age. This was the
task to which he devoted the last years of his literary

power, and much of his work hereafter had the promulgation of this idea for its object.

Of similar import was the book of 1888, " Oannes according to Berosus," his theme in this instance being the history of the culture of the Chaldeans at the hands of Oannes, a Triton of the Persian Gulf, as related by Berosus, priest of Bel's Temple in the time of Alexander the Great; it gives its meaning according to the doctrine of correspondences, and argues therefrom its inspired nature.

Wilkinson's books brought him interesting correspondents, and " Oannes " was specially provocative in this way. Among these letters was one from " your affectionate and indebted Westland Marston." He wrote on July 11, 1888, " Oannes (I thought before I found you make the same suggestion, that he was nominally, and more than nominally, akin to the Evangelist Ἰωάννησ) has quite absorbed me. Whether derived from the earliest Word or not, there is no doubt, I think, that all ancient legends and mythologies were correspondences to (and from ?) the original Bible. I remember even in the mythology of Ancient Mexico (a remote region where its symbols seem unlikely to have penetrated), there is a striking adumbration both of the Lord and the devil, and the Mexicans were looking forward to the advent of the former (?) as the Jews were to that of the Messiah. A literature of Divine Revelations in some measure leavening the Universe in the spiritual verity of which the unity of all languages (one day to be established) is externally the type. A thousand thanks for this most interesting book, which, besides its general theme, arrests one, almost on every page, by some pregnant hint or suggestion." It met also with a warm expression of approval from Professor Sayce.

In 1888 Wilkinson collected all the information possible about Jasper Swedenborg, Bishop of Skara, and father of the more famous Emanuel Swedenborg, which originally appeared as an article in *The New Church Magazine*, but was reprinted for private circulation. This was an act of piety which he thoroughly enjoyed.

" The Soul is Form and doth the Body make " followed in 1890. This was a return to the subject of the lectures of 1848 and of " The Human Body and its Connexion with Man " of 1851 ; but now the doctrine of Correspondences is more plainly stated ; the anatomy is treated briefly ; its application is the confessed object of the work. Concentrating his attention upon the interdependence of two organs, Wilkinson was able to deal with them at greater length. He himself described the book as treating of " the less known functions and Spiritual Correspondences of the heart and lungs."

A letter to Dr Theobald during this year shows well how essential was the part which Correspondence played in Wilkinson's method of thought. With him it was no question of how far illustration may be used for purposes of argument; visible things were to him more than types of things invisible; they were, rather, the actual presentation of things unseen and outside our present ken, but capable of yielding direct instruction by the use of the Key of Correspondence.

" I am not in agreement with your dear Uncle's Psychology. The word *Emotions* belongs to an age, the present, in which religious states are transient or passing. Emotions are ultimate states of the Will manifested to the senses; the last efflorescences of affections. The affections are the direct continuations of the Will of Ruling Love; the articles of which the Will is the heart; the great constant channels which carry the life of the Will through the whole Man; and he is what they are. The emotions are manifested occasional ends of the affections."

" Religion with man must reside in the Will, or it is nowhere else. There residing, it is a new conscience, formed divinely by truth of doctrine committed to life—lived. Faith and conscience are here at one, or the same thing. Man directly makes Will, faith and conscience, ' by acting sincerely, justly and faithfully ' under the Lord's guidance in all his day's works or duties. He acknowledges that it is all the Lord's mercy which enables him to do this, but he does not in the same

I

sense *feel* it ; but feels, and is to feel, that he is doing it himself. Otherwise he would be a Nothing. I do not believe in ' the sense of infinite dependence,' (here in a pencil note is added "*I do,* but the word ' absolute ' is better than ' infinite ' '") or that Angel or Man ever had it. The sense of independence of God, constantly given by Him, but intellectually acknowledged to be only an appearance necessary for finite existence, seems more true."

On June 3, 1892, Wilkinson wrote to his daughter Mrs Pertz on his eightieth birthday.

" Your strong hand-writing and dear heart-writing do me good, and make me grateful on my eightieth birthday. It is a long life to review, and God the Lord is merciful. I have to thank and sing praises to Him for His mercies beyond all deserts. She who is with Him gave me dear children, and brought them up in virtue and enlightenment, and they and grandchildren and great-grandchildren are round me. May we be all ' the people of His pasture and the sheep of His hand ! ' "

In this, his eighty-first year, Wilkinson produced two books. The first, " The African and the True Christian Religion, his Magna Charta," a study in the writings of Emanuel Swedenborg, " was yet another of his arguments in favour of widely-spread primæval knowledge, as well as a plea for a fuller recognition of the Negro's brotherhood to the white man." The second, " Epidemic Man and

his Visitations " was, in his own words to a friend
" intended to assert that all our Diseases are our own
deeds, confronting us, by conversion of forces into
bodily ruin and planetary catastrophe " ; a doctrine
which, if it could but gain general acceptance, would
immensely encourage " physiological righteousness."

On August 8, 1893, Wilkinson suffered another
great loss in the death of his eldest daughter, Mrs
Pertz. During her widowhood she had lived much
with her father and had acted as mistress of his home.
She was a woman of great understanding; of great
will power, often unsuspected under her gentleness
and self-forgetfulness. Her loss was a grievous
one and shook Wilkinson severely. Two grand-
daughters, Emma and Florence Pertz, however,
were left to brighten and comfort the home.

Journeys were now difficult, but Wilkinson was
still able to visit his daughters at Pontrilas Court
and at Sevenoaks. He also enjoyed staying with
the Countess de Noailles at Eastbourne, who shared
his views on many subjects, and who to the end
remained his friend and patient.

Still, though strength was failing, the will was
firm; and the literary output continued, though
it cost more toil, and was less rapidly executed;
but it showed no loss of power or of force and felicity
in expression.

During this year the Reverend Professor Tafel,
a friend of many years' standing died, with whom

Wilkinson had been closely associated in the translation and editing of Swedenborg's work on " The
Brain," which Tafel ultimately dedicated to his
friend. Wilkinson had revised the proofs page by
page, being probably the only Englishman of sufficient
knowledge at once of Swedenborg and Anatomy
to undertake the task. The friendship thus formed
was a close one, and its close (in so far as death could
close any friendship of Wilkinson's) saddened him.
He remained in correspondence with Mrs Tafel for
years.

The following letter is characteristic of the man at
this time, full of old memories, failing somewhat
in bodily strength, but with a firm and faithful
hold upon present interests [1] :—

" Thank you for the beautiful ferns and flowers.
My fifty-sixth Wedding Day has been peaceful,
and full of memories. All of you are the garland
given me by that faithful and excellent wife.

" Dr Dudgeon has just been here, and finds me
on the mend. I have a bronchial attack ; but it
is yielding to his treatment. To-day I am down
earlier than usual.

" Come when you can, but do not fatigue yourself.

" Our international relations are distressful. We
are necessarily an isolated nation. An island with
vast present possessions must be. We don't easily
form alliances, in order that we may not be re-

[1] Letter to his daughter, Mrs F. C. Mathews, January 5, 1896.

sponsible for concerns not our own. Hence we are
thought proud and haughty, and every power has
a pluck at us. And we are a peculiar people, I
believe in a good sense. All these are dislikeable
points. May the Lord of Nations make us just and
honest, and brave therein ! "

There was something of the spirit of this last
paragraph, a spirit of statesmanship rather than
of politics, in his next book, " The Affections of
Armed Powers : a plea for a School of little Nations."
He dedicated it to his son-in-law Mr Frank Mathews,
with whom a strong intellectual sympathy and
mutual esteem ever existed.

Another book of this year (1897) was the subject of much thought and of considerable study.
Wilkinson himself said that " it had loomed in his
mind for fifty years of cogitative thought." As
far back as 1890, writing to his friend Professor
Victor Rydberg, to acknowledge his book " Fädernas
Gudasaga," he said that he had long meditated
a spiritual commentary upon " Voluspå," and adds,
" Remains of good, tenderly remembered from
innocent times, are the uncorrupted dwellings of
the Lord in men, and the fresh starting points
of salvation." And, on another occasion, he wrote,
" I read almost all the Norse mythology into an
internal sense, corresponding to the Revealed
internal sense." Wilkinson was deeply learned in
Icelandic, Swedish, and German Mythology, and had

contemplated a thorough treatment of the whole subject, but he fell back upon " Voluspå " as within his limits of power and time. How earnestly he pursued his theme, the following extract from a letter to Mr Iòn a Hjaltalin will show. " My effort, which must be merely tentative and ground-breaking, to find whether the seed can be sown upon it, so as to come towards revelation, is of a different kind (to some previous etymological considerations). All I can say is that as I proceed, praying that some of the wise and simple little children above may be sent to open my mind, I do make progress, and find a connected chain, or a road with good bridges, in parts of the ' Voluspå ' which seem most abrupt. And, for all I discern, the Prophecy needs no altering or the order of its *chants*."

" The Book of Edda called ' Voluspå,' a study in its scriptural and Spiritual Correspondences " deals with the full internal interpretation of the Prophecy of the Vala. The work is prettily dedicated to his granddaughters, " My free comrades in life and work," as the studies of a grandfather.

There is some special quality of wear and work in that generation of old people which is now very rapidly disappearing, the children of the men who broke Napoleon at Waterloo. Whether their children, in their turn, will astonish their descendants by force and longevity is questionable. But it is certain that the generation to which Wilkinson belonged was blessed with a continuance of force beyond what is ordinary. In them was the saying, " Those whom the Gods love die young," explained as meaning, " Those whom the Gods love are young until they die." But, though it appears postponed, there is a period for them too; and, one by one, we see these " grand old men " gathered to their fathers. Slowly and in the main without suffering, Wilkinson realized physically that he was nearing his end. " I am weak *rather*, but fairly well," he wrote,[1] " and I believe that if I had faith to begin I could get on with my writing. But I fear I am ' giving in,' and making my entry into the eighty-fifth room of existence into an excuse for being served instead of serving." But he was far indeed from complaint.[2] " I am now very infirm, and can hardly do anything of a day's work. This was also the reason of my long silence on which your ladies commented. I am weak and poorly. So you must make allowance for me, and, if I can write but seldom, know that I value intercourse with your mind highly, as I have always done, since I knew you. My Grand-daughters, after a long German tour, are now at home for the winter, and I have every blessing that old age requires. They are treasures."

Of " that which should accompany old age, as Honour, love, obedience, troops of friends," nothing

[1] Letter to Mrs Ruxton, August 8, 1896.
[2] Letter to Mr Thomson, October 28, 1896.

was lacking—nor was the outlook into the future a doubting one. He wrote to a friend[1] who told him of a dream concerning one " gone before."

" It is the beginning of a world of Revelations, of which the last, to those who can receive it, is permanence and Heaven. How such assurances should chasten Churchyard theology, and teach that the days of death are short for everyone and that resurrection out of the body begins immediately! And then that the Use of having been born in nature shines out before good spirits as soon as they awaken. The dead world has been the A.B.C. and forerunner of the living world: the dead Sun of the living Sun: no metaphor or parable, but a Spiritual Orb with the Lord God Almighty veiled in its glory. It is lovely to think, lovelier to *know*, that the landscapes of heaven are peopled with trees, with birds, with animals, and that all these are divine Uses and continual scriptures of instruction, varying from state to state."

In 1898 Wilkinson found great pleasure in the marriage of his elder granddaughter, Miss Emma Leonora Pertz, to Mr E. J. Payne, author of " The History of the New World called America." He was a learned and highly cultured man, congenial in tastes to his new relations. It was an event which threw a cheerful gleam of light upon Wilkinson's last months.

[1] Letter to Mrs Roberts, May 20, 1897.

There remained one more piece of literary work for the full brain and tired hand of the man of eighty-seven. The last book, like the first, contributed to the Swedenborgian interpretation of revelation. The preface to Blake's "Songs of Innocence and Experience" was dated July 9, 1839 when Wilkinson was but twenty-seven years old; he dated his dedication of "Isis and Osiris in the Book of Respirations; Prophecy in the Churches; In the Word; God with Us; The Revelation of Jesus Christ," to Dr Alfred Wiedemann, Professor in the University of Bonn, on September 16, 1899. In the first he quoted Swedenborg as giving the only possible explanation of Blake's inspiration: in the last he demonstrates by the Doctrine of Correspondences the internal meaning of an ancient Egyptian scroll. He had passed away before the latter, the last of a long series, had reached his hand.

Less than a week before his death he wrote to his daughter, Mrs F. C. Mathews, to celebrate her birthday. He said, "I am well and surrounded by your bounties. . . . I had hoped to have my little Book, 'Isis and Osiris in the Book of Respirations' on your table; but it will come to you later. Inasmuch as the fresh air is strength, my unlearned Tract, for such it is, may carry you both through some journeys of sight and thought, ending in new regions. Since boyhood I have been a student of spirit, material and substantial, and it is for me a sacred continuation unbroken to the end of the chain."

There was nothing violent in the manner of his death : the strength of body failed and the spirit returned to God who gave it. Surrounded by all whom he loved best on earth, this lifelong searcher for the unknown stepped into the Valley of the Shadow, nothing doubting that the comfort of the Shepherd's rod and staff would be with him, confidently expecting the company and enlightenment of those who had gone before him to the Home of the Father.

.   .   .   .   .   .

It should be possible for one who has enjoyed acquaintance with Garth Wilkinson, with his friends, with his many published writings, with his most intimate private correspondence, to indicate some cardinal points in his nature around which his motives and activities were wont to revolve. Three such convenient points for studying his character seem to be his mysticism, his transcendentalism and his impatience.

Mysticism is a word too often rendered obscure by misuse. It should not be used to signify mystery or vagueness of metaphysical aim. It is here used of the sense of the immanence, or indwelling presence, of God in the nature of man. Such a sense is seldom entirely lacking in individuals, and it would appear to play an essential part in the scheme of every religious system. The mystic is one who possesses this sense in a high degree and cultivates it as the most noble part of his being. The Christian mystic is one who cultivates this sense by constant reference to the incarnation of Christ, the doctrine which deduces from the human nature of the Divine Man a promise of an increasing godliness for himself and his fellows. This sense was strongly marked in Dr Wilkinson: it found expression more frequently and more fully as his nature developed, and as the aim of his life-work defined itself before him. The central importance of the Incarnation is dwelt upon with growing insistence in both his books and his letters. He himself was used to reserve the word Theology for the Word of God communicated in revelation; but his own message, consisting as it did throughout of teaching with regard to the respective natures of God and man and of the relations and duties consequent upon those natures, can scarcely be classified as other than " theological " according to the accepted use of terms.

A deep religious instinct showed itself early in his life, in the musings and night-terrors, and in the paradoxical rebellions of his childhood, which occupy a relatively large space in his fragment of Autobiography. From the end of the time covered by that short document, we have little evidence of his inner life until he began the copious letter-writing which lasted to his death. But, he confesses himself, in his intimate letters to his *fiancée*, as having passed through a period of doubt in his early manhood, and even speaks of himself as having been a "rank skeptic" during some of that time. It is not a rare experience of youth; not seldom it points rather to immature and necessarily unsatisfactory attempts to fathom the deepest subjects than to any mental attribute which will work permanent effect upon character. It was so in his case.

A new faith in God and a new human love reached Garth Wilkinson almost simultaneously in his introduction to the writings of Swedenborg and his attachment to the lady who became his wife; and his progress in both may be traced in letters neither fitted nor intended for quotation, but which make it plain that each of these elements helped the other in his new awakening. The force of this fresh grasp of his relation to his Maker and to his fellows endured and increased throughout Wilkinson's life, and his character appears to have grown deeper and gentler as the years went by, under the influence of the two collateral factors. For the rest, it will suffice to point out here that all knowledge which came in his way and all experience which life brought to him were sublimated into contributions toward the comprehension and cultivation of the divine in man.

The essential part which faith in the Godhead and manhood of Christ played in Wilkinson's mysticism, and the attitude of that mysticism toward pantheism, will be best considered in a chapter devoted to his religious position as a pupil of his great master Swedenborg.

Transcendentalism, again, is a term which needs careful definition before use. It has at least three different significations. Firstly, it was applied to a school of philosophy most commonly associated with the name of Kant. Secondly, the term was tacked on to a dreary religious sect of theists who affirmed nothing but the existence of a God and promulgated a dry optimism concerning the future of our race. Thirdly, the name was applied, (no man knowing wherefore, and themselves least of all) to an ill defined intellectual and religious movement among certain distinguished New Englanders of whom Everett, Emerson and Channing may be named as prominent, in the first half of the nineteenth century. Somebody has defined the movement as " a pilgrimage from the idolatrous world of creeds and rituals to the Temple of the Living God in the soul ; " and it is not easy to include all those who claimed to march under its banner within any stricter limitation. Indeed, limits, formularies and definitions were their abhorrence.

No reader or acquaintance of Wilkinson's could be in any danger of classing him among the philo-

sophic Transcendentalists.   His own attitude towards
the Kantian school is very clearly displayed in the
Introductory Remarks with which he prefaced
his translation from Swedenborg, " Outlines of a
Philosophical Argument of the Infinite " (1847).

" In a word the upshot of Transcendentalism
was to regard all sensation, knowledge and thought
as subjective, and to make the individual believe
all the manifestations of God, nature or humanity
which are made to his mind, as so many presentations
of his own being. In this way, each man becomes
shut in the case of an opaque and impenetrable
selfhood, which not only absorbs and destroys
all outward truth, but makes it impossible to
have any confidence in the existence of our
brother man. To accept these consequences is the
manner in which Transcendentalism has answered
scepticism ! "

It is clear, too, that the Theistic Transcendentalists
of our classification could claim no adherent in
Wilkinson. By a process of exclusion, therefore,
we are left to consider his position among the last
of our list.

Perhaps the only comprehensive bond which
would gain recognition among those whom for
brevity we will call the New England Transcendentalists was freedom from traditional ties. Each
enjoyed content while he followed individual conscience by such light of revelation as he had ; and

each disclaimed all fettering limitations which at any time marred that content. There was no Church, no Brotherhood, no organization among them : they were men and women seeking Spiritual freedom by the light of conscience. In this alone they shared sympathy : by this alone they recognized each other in the world over which they were spread. It was therefore quite consistent with his Transcendentalism that Wilkinson should claim some measure of theo-pneustic inspiration for Emanuel Swedenborg, that he should at the same time be a Communicant of the Church of England, and that he should regard both Swedenborg and the Church of England as Divine, but temporary, provisions for man in his present state. But he held that the Creator transcended all his creatures, and that new revelations of the Nature and Will of the Creator were constantly occurring, both through the medium of Correspondences and otherwise ; and that such revelations were to be constantly expected and acknowledged.

This faculty for pushing forward towards the unknown, this readiness to accept new light from any source, caused uneasiness amongst those who were his best wishers and most competent admirers. Thus, Emerson, writing of Wilkinson soon after his own second visit to England, in 1847, gave him encouragement high and stately, but added a warning in clear words :

" Wilkinson, the editor of Swedenborg, the anno-tator of Fourrier, and the champion of Hahnemann, has brought to metaphysics and to psychology a native vigour, with a catholic perception of relations, equal to the highest attempts, and a rhetoric like the armoury of the invincible knights of old. There is in the action of his mind a long Atlantic roll not known except in deepest waters, and only lacking what ought to accompany such powers, a manifest centrality. If his mind does not rest in immovable biases, perhaps the orbit is larger, and the return is not yet ; but a master should inspire a confidence that he will adhere to his convictions, and give his present studies always the same high place." (Emerson. *English Traits*. Literature).

There was in the earlier days of Dr Wilkinson's conscious powers, a time when he was still unversed in exercising them. It was difficult to display manifest centrality, to avoid a suggestion of giddiness, while new vistas of possibility spread themselves at each point of view. Confidence that he would adhere to his convictions was possible to friends who knew the inherent rash honesty of their man : but there had to be a season when the man was himself uncertain which of his then " present studies " would absorb him and exhibit itself as his pre-dominant objective. It would have appalled an ordinary inquirer concerning Swedenborgianism to read such expressions as Dr Wilkinson wrote to

his friend Mr Henry James, when he was writing
of his lectures (October 26, 1848) :—

" I begin to find that the age is indeed ripe for all
that can be told it ; only it is in that degree of
childish weakness, that the Manner is indispensable
to the matter ; the terrible novelties must be said
pretty, and then they excite nothing but pleasant
tastes. . . . I cannot have anything but hope
of the whole world, because I see everywhere either
earnest search for truth, as in France, or steady
obedience, as here ; and this ass, or that horse, will
alike serve for the august riders into the earthly
and the heavenly Jerusalems.

" This matter of growth is with me a most interesting fact, as it places each age in freedom, and eman-
cipates all children from the overweening dominion
of their best and gentlest predecessors. A Swedenborg is good and great, but the babies of the new
generation are born to estates just fresh from God,
and which Swedenborg could not even conceive.
All men are new creations and want new creations
wherein and whereby to live."

The return of the forecast is not yet. Forty
years have passed, and the New Church has not
yet transcended and outgrown the teaching of
Swedenborg. A series of bright visions, born of
new illumination, cannot be profitably measured
by the foot-rule or tested by laws of perspective.
The years were to teach, as is their way, that

K

illumination is a difficult possession to transfer, even by the most persuasive of manners. Experience was to clip the wings of optimism, but never to break them. A carefully limited field of work had yet to be defined and followed. Plodding work, patient reiteration, a brilliant versatility, indomitable perseverance, were the qualities which forty years were to educate and spend.

This " exorbitance," this tendency to fling off red-hot fragments from the periphery at unexpected angles, was not, even while it was most in action, altogether hidden from the man himself : and he was working towards a true consistency of aim and expression. In his next letter to the same friend he writes (November 22, 1848), relative to some untraced communication, to *The Harbinger* of New York :—

" I should rather that my paper on Correspondence appeared without my name : it is a transition paper, and I have already outgrown it in some parts. Besides, I regret now all that I have printed, except only my Translations. Please God, better and graver things are to come from me than what have been seen."

But transcendentalism, in the sense of eagerness and readiness to discard limitations and to outgrow the partial views of yesterday, remained the chief and not least lovable traits in the man's nature while he remained in sight.

Closely allied to this was the third of Wilkinson's noteworthy characteristics, one which, for lack of a better name I have called *impatience*. It was impatience of no ignoble order. The man was so seized of the nearness and reality of the unseen spiritual world, so desirous of revelation, so anxious for " Influx," that he suffered what amounted to intellectual torment. Was there no prayer in answer to which the veil would rise ? Was there a trumpet call which would raze the dividing wall and leave a practicable breach for the besieger ? Could he find, even in unlikely places, some overlooked hint, the secret key to the locked door ? The ultimate object of his search was the coming down from heaven of the New Jerusalem, the appointed hour of which Swedenborg (and the Gospel long before Swedenborg) had proclaimed as beyond human ken. In the early days of his adoption of the Sweden-borgian revelations, it seemed to him that the time could not be long, and the service of standing and waiting was proportionately severe. He sought for signs which should support the urgency of his hope, and sought them in strange places. There was no path along what are regarded as the boundaries of the unknown down which his footsteps might not be traced : mesmerism, hypnotism, spiritualism, with its apparatus of rappings, mediums, and clairvoyance, healing as an immediate divine gift, Fourrierism and T. L. Harrisism—he explored them all, with this impatience of his quest to drive him, and discovered each to be a *cul-de-sac* in the maze before he abandoned it.

But if this impatience was not ignoble, it was quite unscientific. To educate the eye into that of a Seer may make it the eye of the Poet, but will never make it the eye of the Scientist. As Coleridge has said, " Poetry is not the antithesis to prose, but to Science " ; Science demands " the *patience* for uncorrelated fragments, the endurance of incompleteness." The uncorrelation of fragments was the very subject of Garth Wilkinson's impatience ; incompleteness was the very last thing which he found it easy to endure. His message, couched in terms of speculation, suffered. For, though he passed his youth in days when speculation was popular and, was, in consequence, gladly heard, the years of his matured powers were years of scientific expansion and advance, and a message conceived in hostility to science met deaf ears or, at best, a partial welcome. The world now rejects enthymemes and demands scientific proof of the first two figures of your syllogism before it will examine the third. But if from one point of view he appears as the last of the Transcendentalists, as the voice of one crying in the wilderness to a small congregation, there is another view equally possible and more just. Age, inevitable disappointment, and, above all, spiritual growth, quieted the impatience we speak of. But, if he realized that the mills of God grind slowly, Garth Wilkinson suffered no doubt as to the thoroughness of their working or the nature of their work. It might be that the coming of the New Jerusalem could not be hastened, that it could not even be discerned as nearer, within the lifetime of man ; but it could be furthered, the paths could be made straight and the crooked places plain : and to this task he addressed his pen almost literally to his last hour. He found his task in the demonstration of correspondences : he pursued and enriched it from his great store of varied learning. One had spoken of him as being " half a century before the intelligence of the world." [1] If the estimate is correct, the fruit of his mind and spirit will be found ready for the taste and appetite of a generation who knew not the man on earth : they would enjoy the banquet the better for the presence of their host !

But he himself was under no illusion as to the amount of acceptance accorded to him, and it troubled him little if his listeners were few : his labour was, so far as in him lay, to make them fit. Late in his life he wrote to a friend : [2] " In a few thousand years, the coming of the New Jerusalem may be discernible in love to God and love to man : but a good many cycles of World-overthrow may be gone through

[1] Letter from Dr Pearson, April 7, 1878.
[2] Letter to Mr John Marten, December 23, 1893.

in the interval." He has clearly learned the lesson of patience as regards his great hope. Writing, at the age of eighty-five, to his friend Mr John Thomson, of Candorrat, Glasgow, a bookseller, he says, (January 17, 1898): " Do not attribute carelessness to me for not writing to you earlier : I have been so anxiously working at my unpopular book-making." He was not seeking his own glory.

Emerson wrote in his lecture on " Swedenborg, or the Mystic " : " Swedenborg printed these scientific works in the ten years from 1734 to 1744, and they remained from that time neglected : and now, after their century is complete, he has at last found a pupil in Mr Wilkinson, in London, a philosopher critic, with a co-equal vigour of understanding and imagination comparable only to Lord Bacon's, who has restored his master's buried books to the day, and transferred them, with every advantage, from their forgotten Latin into English, to go round the world, in our commercial and conquering tongue. This startling reappearance of Swedenborg, after a hundred years, in his pupil, is not the least re-markable fact in his history. Aided, it is said, by the munificence of Mr Clissold, and also by his literary skill, this piece of poetic justice is done. The admirable preliminary discourses with which Mr Wilkinson has enriched these volumes, throw all the contemporary philosophy of England into shade, and leave me nothing to say on their proper ground." The praise is high but not unmeasured, *Laetus sum laudari me abs te, pater, a laudato viro*, but there is a praise still higher, of which those who love him trust that he may be found worthy. Garth Wilkinson esteemed himself a " steward of the mysteries," and " it is required of a steward that he shall be found faithful."

CHAPTER II

GARTH WILKINSON's religion was the centre of his life. All problems which presented themselves to him were referred to it; his motives emanated from it. He was early introduced to Christianity and revelation as presented by Swedenborg, and never did those doctrines fall upon ground better suited for their reception and development. Probably with small thought concerning the momentous meaning of his action, Wilkinson threw himself at once into a thorough and exhaustive study of " the writings," and was soon recognised as a born translator. He was, indeed, from the first more than a careful renderer of his original from one language to another. We have seen in the preceding chapter how early in his task he was struggling for a mastery of those *nuances* of expression which raise the drudge into the artist, and open out the genius of an author to the mind of those who see him in his new dress. As in the case with most conscientious work, the effort brought more than a creditable fulfilment of the immediate task in hand. Not only did Wilkinson gain an intimacy

152

with the *ipsisima verba* of Swedenborg, probably
peculiar to himself in his own generation ; he acquired
in addition to this a readiness of expression, a facility
and virility of literary workmanship, which could
not have failed, if used upon themes less unpopular
than those he followed, to redound to his fame and
profit.   But these were not what he sought.

A vision of the reality and nearness of spiritual
life through the exegesis of Swedenborg, was for him
a call to his life-work.   What he himself saw must
be rendered visible to all men to the best of his
power.   Having graduated through translation
into learning, he found himself possessed of gifts
which made his pen a valuable weapon.   Armed
with it, he threw himself into a life of use, and
became the most versatile and original of Swedenborg's disciples.   His enthusiasm of spirit and power
of mind, were, indeed, so fitted to the task of his
self-devotion that to some he appeared more in the
position of a reincarnation than a follower of his
master.   Swedenborg, buried in manuscript under
the dust of a century's neglect, seemed, to some at
least, to speak again.   As Mr Emerson said [1] :—
" This startling re-appearance of Swedenborg, after
a hundred years, in his pupil, is not the least
remarkable fact in his history."

A large shelf full of books are a public testimony
to the zeal with which Wilkinson utilized his talent

---

[1] Representative men : " Swedenborg, or the Mystic."

in promulgating the truth as he saw and held it. For him, the writings of Swedenborg enshrined the latest word of revelation vouchsafed to man. As he traced the word of God in the Sagas and in the hieroglyphic writings of ancient Egypt in the past, so, too, he confidently expected further revelation which should supersede the message of Swedenborg, in its turn, in that future when man was educated to receive it. For the present, however, he must labour to have that message heard and heeded. The works in which he sought that end have been enumerated and characterized in the foregoing chapter. A full critical appreciation of their scope and execution would here be out of place : it will be enough to say that they naturally classify themselves as textual, explanatory and developmental. The textual works, consisting of translations and editions of Swedenborg's writings, are the hand-books and classics of the New Church at the present day, and are little likely to be superseded while the English language lasts. Within the explanatory and developmental classes fall Wilkinson's Introductions to the several works which he translated and edited, and also the vast amount of brilliant illustration which he bestowed upon the far-reaching doctrine of Correspondences, in which he traced examples of mystical correspondence in the early writings of the race and in the occurrences of his own day.

But the effect of religion can only be partially estimated by a consideration of a man's published works. Its influence upon conduct and upon character are fully seen and known only to the Maker of man. Upon this subject it must suffice to say that in his personal life, Wilkinson consistently regulated his conduct by the lofty creed which he professed, and that, having served his generation faithfully and unremittingly, he fell on sleep.

Those who need an exposition of Swedenborg's doctrines or an estimate of his value among the religious teachers of the world will find them elsewhere, and not least satisfactorily in the works of Wilkinson. We are here rather concerned to define the place of Wilkinson among his disciples, and to give, so far as may be in his own words, his views upon the subject to which he devoted his life and by which he regulated his conduct.

The most important question which can be propounded to a Christain is that which Christ asked his immediate followers: " Whom say *ye* that I am ? " The answer in Wilkinson's case is very distinct.[1] " The Doctrine of the Divine Humanity is clearly the highest doctrine of Heaven. The glorification of that Humanity is by analogy the rule of all progress, of all movement toward goodness. There is not a single sphere of knowledge but is hollow and unsubstantial if the recognition of that doctrine

[1] Letter to Mr Henry James, December 2, 1846.

is not in it. It reconciles the Idealist to nature and the Materialist to God. In a word, it gives poor humanity a new and everlasting root in a fresh covenant; and is emphatically Religion. It is a doctrine which I hope my dear friend will spend and be spent for. The commonest knowledge and the merest obeisance to duty best illustrate it. He who makes no excursion into the sciences (using the term in its modern limited sense) may find in his own home here a deeper insight into Creation, and windows more pellucid and truly crystalline, than all the vagueness of self-sought things can otherwise afford him. In a word, if you be so minded, there is no need to study anything less than humanity for the confirmation of the Divine Humanity; least of all to oppress the memory with the broken pieces into which the creation is every day reduced by the *savans*."

Writing to the same friend, he says[1] : "I am sure I am a much more outside person than you, and with much less faith; thus I cleave to the historical, as a Romanist to his dolls; and when you talk of *the* Christ, I feel pained at the definite article, because it makes Christ Himself—the only one I know of—indefinite. . . . I cannot make History movable to please anybody; and, as to what has occurred I imagine its fact value to be inalienable. . . . The full influence of the letter is as necessary as that of the Spirit."

[1] June 1, 1849.

Our last quotation on this vital point is evidently in answer to a letter which is no longer extant. However it shows Wilkinson's attitude toward the doctrine of the Incarnation so distinctly that it must find place here.

"[1] In your letter to me, I think you scientifically wrong in evaporating the personality of Christ in order to procure the universality of *the* Christ. It is against nature, as much as against God. The " old superstitious standpoint " is indeed the only one; the philosophical ' mathematical point ' is no substitute for it. Life and limb, I adhere to the former, and find it more and more confirmed to me by all my studies and thoughts. You seem to think that the human existence of Christ is not his Divine Existence also; and that the six-foot measure of His person plainly demonstrates His finiteness., I regard it differently, and see in the whole universe nothing but a provision for giving Omnipresence, Omnipotence and Omniscience to perfections, and not to sizes. But I will reserve what I have to say on this until I have read your book."

St John's avowal, in Browning's " Death in the Desert," is not more definite :—

> " I say the acknowledgment of God in Christ
> Accepted by thy reason, solves for thee
> All questions in the earth and out of it;
> And has so far advanced thee to be wise."

[1] Letter to Mr Henry James, March 22, 1850.

The discussion between the friends did not end here. We shall meet later with a continuation of it on Mr James' part.

Holding these strong views upon the Incarnation, it follows that Wilkinson held his Bible as directly and fully inspired. He held also that much which is obscure in the Bible had been specially revealed to Emanuel Swedenborg, and that the Word in its fulness was not granted to those who did not avail themselves of this help. The relation in which he viewed his Bible and " the writings " is compendiously stated in the following letter[1] :—

" I am weak and unable to complete a little work I have on hand, so within the last fortnight I have read through Swedenborg " *De Coelo et Inferno*," in the original. I regard it as the Law-Revealing Sinai of the Lord's Second Advent. I do not regard Swedenborg's works as *subsidiary* to the Word, but as capable of being absorbed into it: so that the internal Word will be all in all; those Works from without and from within subsisting to declare it."

" This is not the place," he says in 1897,[1] to do more than affirm that the Lord has opened the Word to Emanuel Swedenborg by the revelation to him of the internal sense within the letter which consists of correspondences." Further statements of

---

[1] Letter to Mr John Thomson, February 1, 1896.
[2] Preface to " Voluspâ," p. ix.

Wilkinson's views as to the relation which of Swedenborg's works bear to the Bible, is given us in another letter to the same friend.[1]

"There is, indeed, more in the Psalms than Swedenborg saw, and than any man but God-man, the speaker of them, will ever see. But Swedenborg alone has been commissioned to open the Psalms, by being ordered by God-man to reveal the whole doctrine of the Incarnation. That is what makes Jesus Christ alone the opener of the Psalms. They treat primarily of the whole state of Jesus, born a natural man of Mary, born a Divine-Natural man from God from Heaven, conquering universal Hell, as man must conquer his own particular self-hell ; and His (Jesus') conquest in fight against temptations, enabling Man again to have free-will ; Jesus creating the Divine-Natural Degrees in Himself, and therewith becoming one with the Divine-Spiritual and celestial Degrees, and thus one with the Father.

"The Psalms recount all the horrors and terrible states which Jesus' living with hell testifies. How do we know this ? By the last chapter of Luke, in which Jesus, on the way to Emmaus made it known to mankind, 'These are the words which I spake unto you while I was yet with you, how that all things must be fulfilled which are written in the law of Moses and the Prophets and *the Psalms*

[1] Letter to Mr John Thomson, March 14, 1899.

concerning me.' None of this has come home to Jesus until Swedenborg doctrinally opened it."

The opinions which Wilkinson held upon the " infallibility " or degree of inspiration granted to Swedenborg in his various writings is very carefully stated in the following long letter written in answer to an inquiry on the subject from a friend in America[1] :—

" I appreciate your difficulties about the ' infallibility ' of the writings of Swedenborg; I mean about the claim of it for the theological writings. For myself I dismiss the word, infallibility, into the sphere of Papacy. Swedenborg never said he was infallible. What he implied was that he was over-ruled by the Lord—his own will evidently capable of the obedience necessary to write the internal sense of the Word, as it could be received by Mankind. No angel helped him; on the contrary, the Angels often told him what poor matter he was writing from their standpoint; and he, guided by the Lord, replied, that it was up to the level of the intelligence of the receptive world in his day. This debasing of the coin of internal truth, by amalgamating it with the copper of the natural man, and so making it hard and substantial to us, though the gold of heaven was interfered with, hardly comes under the word, infallibility. The *use* of the amalgamating process is produced by an infallible Valuer, but the process itself is *accommodation*;

[1] Letter to Mrs Cockerell, May 5, 1890.

and the coming Æon will see more and more than Swedenborg was commissioned to reveal; so that whoso believes in the finality of any statement of the internal sense, will limit the ever advancing glory of the Word. Nevertheless, every stage is the Word of God, and is the internal sense of the Word of God to us; and we cannot be deceived in regarding it as such.

" The Word of God is a various revelation. It is God Himself, He tells us, in the beginning. No man sees or knows it save as the daylight of the divine Sun above the heavens. In the heavens it is the Lord in and with the angels; but as Himself in a definite divine revelation, as a Book also. On Earth it is a written perpetuated Book possessed by man. All through, therefore, the Word has two characters; God's being and property in it; and the loan of it to man. This seems to connect itself with the question How a divine commentary on the Word, like the authoritative explication vouchsafed to and through Swedenborg, is to be taken as itself the Word, and co-real with the Word ? If in any age it is all that man can know of the Word, such Voice of God is the Word to men, external or literal, internal or spiritual; and doctrinal.

" The Word as God is thus separated from the imparted Word as suited by *divine mercy*, and therefore as still infinite, to the state of the heavens and the churches. All authoritative expositions

L

of the Word, are, as Uses, co-real with the Word for our regeneration : they are divinely true and good. No exposition, however, is co-real with the declaration, ' In the beginning was the Word, and the Word was with God, and the Word was God.'

" As to our attitude of acceptance of Swedenborg's infallibility, he himself is dead against it for the men of heaven and the men of earth. In heaven he saw a temple on which was written ' Now it is granted to enter intellectually into the mysteries of faith.' For us on earth he has said, ' Consider what I say with reason, and with reason accept it.' These declarations (which I put in my own words) are incompatible with receiving this author's works with blind faith. Though it must be added that the affirmation or faith of love for what is good and true is the way, truth and life of the needful understanding of the writings of the New Jerusalem. To an Atheist neither of the above permissions or recommendations applies. To him there are no mysteries of faith, and no reception of any spiritual instruction into the breast of reason. He is an infallible selfhood.

" Now, banishing infallibility as a dangerous apoplexy of the active mind, we come to Swedenborg's theological writings, and to their claims. For myself I regard those which he published as divine books. ' The Arcana,' the ' Four Leading Doctrines,' the 'Heaven and Hell,' 'Conjugal Love,' 'Last Judgment,' 'Apocalypse Revealed,' and the rest. For me they are temples of the Holy Spirit. Also 'The Divine Love and Wisdom' and Divine Providence of course. There are errors of information on natural subjects in them, because they were written in the eighteenth century. These are of no consequence to a lover of truth divine. But they have the use of showing infallibility the door —politely.

" With regard to all these works, if you receive in faith and love as much as commends itself to your urgent uses for the bread of life, you do quite enough to be in the great supper, without stumbling over those things which do not commend themselves to you.

" As to the large unpublished works, all readers of them and of the 'Diary' know how greatly luminous and instructive they are. You are absolutely at liberty to receive all the nourishment you can from them. There will be innumerable differences of reception among the readers of these also. Liberty and Rationality will prefer different qualities and quantities in the feast of reason and the flow of soul. Among them I regard the 'Coronis,' 'The Athanasian Creed,' 'The Divine Love and Wisdom' from 'Apocalypse Explained,' and the 'Diarium' and 'Apocalypse Explained' itself, as signal stores for the nourishment and delight of coming Æons.

" Swedenborg's Life for the Use that he was to fulfil has now to be taken into account. He rose from Childhood to Manhood, and through Old Age, as a prepared instrument; ever mounting the divine stairs of Jacob's Ladder; and registered a new sight from the higher light given through the footsteps of an adequate life. The next ages will see, with new rays of truth-perception, that in the long series of pre-theological works from small to large, he was guided and further prepared for the stages to come. A perpetual engrafting of next and next faculties was accomplished on him by the Great Gardener. No infallibility here either; but a constant reception of principles and depths, and rejection of old ways and appearances. So each work was, as it were, a generation in itself, and had to die in its methodic body, that the proximate spiritual might come forth, and continue the ascent. If the so-called scientific works are seen with an open mind, they are spiritual powers and exercises and far off cognitions of theology and of the Divine Word. This is the case with Swedenborg's ' Principles of Chemistry,' in which he has laid the foundation-stone of a godly mineral temple, transparent from top to bottom, which cannot even be dreamt of by the modern commercial medical and culinary chemist. Higher still he mounts in his ' Principia.' His work, (posthumous) on ' Generation ' is ground so new, but closely following anatomy, physiology and living and loving Sex, that it must be an age before any number of readers will want its instructions. Like all the series, it is out of the mind and heart and interests of the end of the Nineteenth Century. It tells the World, as it has never been told before, that we, who object to Divine Revelation, live in an era of mere imagination, and in a feminine age. With respect to this saying let it be observed that no derogation of woman is implied here; but the author means that one half of the soul is predominant, where on the other hand the masculine and feminine forces should be in even ratios, balanced and begetting in the strength of the heavenly conjugment.

" Coming to the ' Economy ' and the ' Animal Kingdom,' the veil of nature grows thinner chapter by chapter, and the correspondence of the organs of the body to the faculties and uses of the Mind and Spirit lightens forth in inductions and deductions and make organization transparent; and instead of the skeleton being seen as in Rontgen's Rays, the spiritual body is visible in the shape in which good and evil will present it after death. All these are therefore preparatory and preliminary treatises on Heaven and Hell. To single one piece of their daylight, we would mention the Doctrine of Respiration, the Life and Union of the Body and the Spirit, and the bodily fulcrum and basis of the emancipation of the intellect as an instrument of regeneration. Space permits no mention of Sweden-

borg's great discoveries in the region of the Brain.
They are the culmination of his natural spiritual
philosophy of the human body.

" Such a series and order as we have sketched,
puts infallibility out of Court. Papacy is a Mummy
in the swathings of its infallibility, and though the
wrappages are many, and the invention curious,
yet the sameness of death and immobility is written
upon the throne on which the Papal Corpse sits.
In the New Church writings, issuing as they do
from the living God, ' behold I make all things new,'
is the eternal protest against the invasion and fixity
of time and space into the Courts of the infinite.
A new heaven and a new earth are our prophecy.

" We come last to say a word on your difficulty
with regard to the " Worship and Love of God ";
a work intermediate between Swedenborg's natural-
spiritual books, and the theological writings. You
would ask, Is the account of Man's first Creation
true ? Can it be relied on ? Crucified by Infallibility, by infallible modern medical scientism, it
can only yield up the ghost. But in and after so
doing, it must be seen as not only natural, but, like
our Lord's body, as a first state of divine natural.
Swedenborg would never affirm his beautiful thought,
of the Two Trees of Life, to be a literal fact. It is
part of a great Mythology which all his previous
works constitute. It belongs to Ark and Emblem,
to Yggdrasil, to the trees of Life in the Word, in

Genesis and Revelation; and received as life-giving by the spiritual intellect, the *Non*-sense of it is the pure mind and reason working out the problems of science with a power given from above. Age by age the sense, quite novel, and quite unselfish and unsensual, will come, when the divine series in the Work is admitted and its place in all the Works from the ' Principles of Chemistry ' to ' The Arcana,' is taken into the account. The Lord's manifestation to Swedenborg in East London was very nigh at hand to him when he wrote this nonsensual Drama and Oratorio.

" It occurs to me to supplement this, which I may perhaps print in *Morning Light*, with the suggestion, that God, well called by Paul the ' Father of Lights,' from the beginning has not helped Mankind directly by imparting to him any natural Sciences. It may be a rule that He reveals to us nothing that we can find out for ourselves. The celestial wisdom of the Adamic Church is no infringement of this order. Its so-called science, summed up in the *knowledge of correspondences*, was of heavenly, not of natural things : and even in primeval Egypt the knowledges were such as could only be attained by Revelation; for they were the absolute spiritual fitnesses of the external worship of the Church to the holy states of the Ancient Men, to God in them. In our remainders from these revelations, the orientation of temples, and other proscripts, are not of natural science, but of primeval revelation. This condition, that we are necessitated to discover all natural scientifics for ourselves is a personal basis of our freewill; for we should soon lose our wholesome love of discovery with its compensated toils, if our second sight, and third sight, and manifold sights of nature were all shown to us gratuitously. And our intelligence would dwindle into animality. With this condition of invention, sciences are for ever and for ever imperfect, and as they can become more and more perfect by our diligence, our understanding minds are created by the daily instruction we receive of our own nothingness. For the end of natural science also is that whatever is good and true in it, is, in spite of all we have just said, a direct gift of the loving economy of the Almighty."

In addition to his great reverence for the works of Swedenborg, Wilkinson was possessed of an affection almost personal for the man who died forty years before he himself was born. There was no detail of Swedenborg's life which was too trivial for careful investigation : he even collected and published all the available material for a memoir of Jasper Svedborg, Bishop of Skara, the Seer's father.

" This is a memorable day," he wrote on January 26, 1896, to his friend Dr Boericke of San Francisco, "the two hundred and sixth anniversary of the birth of Emanuel Swedenborg. Ten days ago, I started

reading 'De Cœlo et Inferno' in Latin, my dear
Samuel H. Worcester's fine Edition; and I finished
the perusal this morning. How much is gained sug-
gestively from the original. . . . To read it is to
know that you will be before the great White Throne.
It is an ' awfully good book.' "

He had the courage of his convictions and would
have no suppression of facts, or eclecticism, where
Swedenborg was concerned.[1]

" I should be grieved if any attempt to exclude the
dreams from your "Monumenta Swedenborgiana"
were to succeed. They are documents which cannot
now be suppressed; and the quietest way in which
they can come forth is in your large Volumes, where
they will assume no disproportionate importance.
Failing that, they will probably issue in a portable,
perhaps in a pamphlet form, and have an unduly
wide circulation. It would be an awkward fact
for the world to handle, if the Society tried to sup-
press the document.

" Those who think Swedenborg mad will think
him no madder for ' The Dreams': those who are
capable of finding him not mad will speedily see in
' The Dreams' a step in the marvellous ladder of
his upraising.

" I remember well when I warmly and earnestly
advocated the publication of the ' Diarium', with
nearly the whole Society against me, many earnest

[1] Letter to Dr Tafel, July 2, 1877.

men were terrified, and one said, ' That book, if published, will disband the Church.' The Lord's Church is not to be disbanded by the whole Truth. I pray you all, fear not; this book, even if it open controversy, will be no stumbling block to any whom it really concerns. The Age is opening fast to a reverent, careful and tolerant study of such phenomena as those indicated in ' The Dreams.'

" May I add, as an old friend and deep well-wisher to the Society, an earnest hope that you will be commissioned at once to proceed to the European part of your work, the publication of all the Documents in the originals. We owe this to the world and to posterity. Make any use you like of this letter."

It may be remembered that in 1836, Wilkinson's first reading at the British Museum was in a History of Philosophers and that he noticed with disapproval the absence of Swedenborg's name from among them. Sixty years later, we find him delivering a firm verdict in the same sense.[1]

" You ask me, who, in my opinion, is the greatest Philosopher of the present time ? My answer is, Emanuel Swedenborg. His writings recognize and adequately demonstrate all the faculties of man, and see them in their connexion from the highest to the lowest as the creations of a Divine love and wisdom.

" The Philosophy lies in the veritable Revelation.

[1] Letter to Mrs Keeley, March 21, 1896.

that human love and wisdom exist in their integrity only in proportion as the rule of higher and inner faculties becomes established in human life, individual and social; so that the relation between God and man is continually established and re-established.

" The two factors of this are God's gifts, both of them, 1. A Word of God, inspired by Him, and plainly full of His Commandments and Laws. 2. A conscience sensitive to the Light of this Word. Obedience is the Use of this conscience in daily Duties.

" These dry statements cover and include a divine Philosophy which has new eyes given to it for the discernment of all things hitherto deemed mysterious. They are windows to which the natural and spiritual worlds freely open.

" This philosophy will not pass away, but with the reformation and regeneration of mankind, age after age, it will become more new and glorious, never forgetting its past, yet living in its present, and not anticipating its future.

" The meaning of this is a divine Church, the religious and secular pulpits of which will grow out of the life of Emanuel's Philosophy."

The high value which Wilkinson attached to Swedenborg's works led him to reverse various generally accepted judgments.[1]

[1] Letter to Miss Marsh, January 28, 1839.

" To my mind the insertion of extracts from Swedenborg spoils the context of any other man— it so completely surpasses all other writing, in its clear-burning tranquility of brightness."

He finds even St Augustine fail when tried by this measure.[1]

" This morning I have read Chapter VII. of St Augustine's Confessions.   He is a sublime Genius, full of great and true intuitions, but which are not on the rational plane.   It is strange to compare him with the substantial lesson of Swedenborg, learnable through him by all the world."

His very love-letters teemed with allusions to Swedenborg.   This is not wonderful between lovers who were studying " The Writings " together, and who sought counsel, warning and encouragement from those pages.[2]

" I am very much pleased with your view of Swedenborg's power of convincing.   It is mild, but how irresistible, like all mild things, or all things which have in them Love, Spiritual mildness.   How do I feel that all my warmth and fury is not strength; that it is weakness!   that if thou or I wish to be strong it must be by renouncing the strength of selfish *passion*, by commencing unselfish *action* ! "

Wilkinson's letters contain very frequent avowals of his religious belief; as a propagandist, he never

---

[1] Letter to Mrs Wilkinson, September 3, 1884.
[2] Letter to Miss Marsh, November 6, 1838.

shrank from testifying. Two examples of this must not be omitted. Writing to Professor Victor Rydberg to acknowledge a present of the Swedish scholar's " Undersökningar i Germanisk Mythologi " in 1890 he says :—

" I have some idea of attempting a review of your Book on some principal points ; perhaps in a little Book. The Northern Mythology has to me a sacred character, and I have long seen that ' Voluspå ' is a tradition of holy things. I am a confirmed and ever more confirmed disciple of Swedenborg, who stands for me in the brain behind ' Heim-skringlas Panna ' as the spirit of the North coming over the whole World ; and as even more than the reunion of the two ends of the Aryan Race— as the Uniter of all the Races under the Divine Word. I say this to declare where I am as your very grateful pupil and admirer."

In the last of his letters to Mr Emerson which have escaped destruction, he is lamenting their failure to meet in London, in spite of many efforts on both sides ; and giving his special reasons for having wished to meet his old friend and helper, he says [1] :—

" In these last days of the Supremacy and Papacy of the Human Mind as Emperor, I wanted so very much to talk to you, and assault you a little, about Swedenborg, for whose proximate extension you

[1] Letter to Mr R. W. Emerson, January 3, 1874.

have done so much. Years ago, when I looked at
him as a great phenomenon mentally, I reckoned
him among the World's great men. Now I see him
as not among (? them) : but as a Divine Functionary,
having in all he does and says a purely spiritual
tendency. So I look upon him as a God-given
pressure of common-sense upon all the relations
of public and private life, which he derives from
the Divine Man, through the Human Heavens,
and Spiritual World, into Humanity in all its bosoms,
and through every stroke of all its businesses. For
this, the coming first, and then the Word and Revelation of the Divine Man is necessary ; and this is
the thing which Swedenborg's mind was opened at
the top to teach.

" In the light of all this I confess myself a Swedenborgian, a name which, a quarter of a century ago,
I should have repugned.

" The opposite to it, involving, as it does, blank
ignorance of the life after death which we are so
soon to enter, appears to me untenable against all
the dearest holiest interests of men and women.

" I know your generosity will excuse my
dogmatism."

Wilkinson's statement that during the later
" fifties " he would have disclaimed being a " Swedenborgian " needs some qualification and brings us
naturally to consider his position as a member of
the " New Church."

The difficulty appears to be one of terms. To the world at large a " Swedenborgian " is a follower of Swedenborg, a member of a religious body terming itself " The New Church." Among those who claimed membership in the New Church were two classes : firstly, those who segregated themselves from other communities and claimed to possess, as a Church, Orders and Sacraments ; these may not unjustly be called Sectarians ; secondly, those who claimed to extract an internal sense from Divine Writ by means of the revelation which they believed to have been granted to Swedenborg and to have been transmitted in " The Writings." These latter did not necessarily find their position inconsistent with membership of other religious bodies or the recognition of the Orders and Sacraments of those bodies. For them the " New Church " was a spiritual body destined to grow in strength and purity by reformation and education due to influx from on high.

It cannot be denied that Wilkinson early in his life was very ready to become, if he did not actually become, a member of the first class which we have defined. He was anxious for example, to be married in a " New Church " place of worship and abandoned his intention partly on account of the inconvenience involved and partly to avoid giving pain to those dear to him.

But shortly before that time we find him writing to his *fiancée* in these terms.[1]

" What you say about the Sacrament is very interesting to me ; and you shall, according to your expressed wish, read me what you have been reading and what Swedenborg says on that subject. I am beginning to feel regrets of a stronger and stronger kind that I attend so little to the forms of Religion and the Church. These regrets, I think, will embody themselves some day in the practice of frequenting Divine Service and partaking of the Holy Sacrament. But at present, from my neglect of these offices during my whole life (save only my school-life, when they were compulsory and far too hardly required), I feel an inability to set myself about performing them." If, as seems likely, the Sacrament of the Eucharist according to the rites of the Church of England is intended, Wilkinson's sectarianism was not, even at its bitterest, very bitter. Seven years later, however, with greater experience of the two classes of the " New Church," he expresses himself with no uncertain sound.[2]

" So Miss —— is in hot water ! We do not wonder at it, and it seems to be a warning to us all not at present to interlock ourselves very closely with any sect or party, and perhaps not to leave that in which we were born. I am tempted to think

[1] To E. A. M., June 17, 1839.
[2] Letter to Mr Henry James, September 18, 1847.

that the times are not free enough to allow men to associate together on mere doctrinal ground, but that if they do this they will coagulate together, or conglutinate, and lose the liberty of action and of thought. This has been my own experience, and I am now, therefore, anxious to belong to no party as a Community but the Church of England, and, by my presence there, to contribute an individual mite toward making that name latitudinarian enough for the millions of diverse spirits who are comprehended under it already. The same advice I tender to others, to be what their fathers were before them, and to labour to improve their ancestral estate. Then, when the better day dawns, the spiritual earth will be fat and fit for the crop which is that day to be sown in it, over all climates. But on this subject, see the 24th Chapter of Matthew, from the 14th to the 28th verse."

This aversion to joining the " sect or party " calling themselves " The New Church " was highly characteristic of him. In every movement he wielded a free lance : his transcendentalism (of the New England type) made him an individualist. Never hesitating to raise voice or use pen in the most unpopular causes, heedless of what obloquy, contumely and controversy he might himself arouse, he yet possessed a caution which saved him from responsibility for what others might say, write or do.

But if the preceding quotation illustrates his

M

attitude towards the "New Church" with which he could not ally himself, that which follows relates to the New Church, the Heavenly Jerusalem whose descent from above was his dream and great desire.[1]

" I cannot doubt that at this day the New Church embraces all that is good and true in all men, creeds and worships ; and that so far as any man is on the road to heaven, so far he is in the New Church, and not in the Old. This certainty gives one a different aim from the simple conversion of congregations from one name to another ; and might tend to make one regard all existing things as forms which might be regenerated into truths without being wrenched from their individual places. How much richer a Church will be which embraces the varieties now shadowed forth by the different Religions and Sects ; than one which tyrannically imposes itself upon all ! In time and through the myriad-fold arm of circumstances wielded by Providence, the fundamental truth of the Divine Humanity and newness of Life, will no doubt be accepted by all Creeds, and will re-animate the Creeds, which will then simply convey the Divine Truths downwards in so many channels fitted to the great and small divisions of the Human Race. And the enlarging charity which shall then appear, will interpret for good, and adopt as of the New Church, many a doctrine which is now repudiated merely from a hard habit of judging

[1] Letter to Mr Henry James, February 28, 1847.

one set of words by another to which it seems heterogeneous."

Wilkinson maintained and even strengthened his connection with the Church of England through the rest of his life, attending its Services and availing himself of its highest act of worship. Probably his readiness to proclaim himself a Swedenborgian in 1874, though he would have repugned the title earlier in his life, was (in part at least) due to a more accurate view of Swedenborgianism in the public mind. His assumption of the name certainly did not connote a deeper Sectarianism. But it must not be inferred that Wilkinson's attitude absolved him from a very active part in those propagandist works of which he approved. The facts are far otherwise. He was for many years from 1839 a working member of the Printing Committee of " The Society for Printing and Publishing the (Theological) writings of Swedenborg," instituted in London 1810; and in 1844, he was largely concerned in founding " The Swedenborgian Association," becoming its first Secretary. The special function of this Association was the editing and translation of Swedenborg's works and manuscripts, " written anteriorly to the opening of his spiritual sight in the year 1745." This was a matter very near to Wilkinson's heart, for he held that his author must be studied chronologically if a man would learn the degrees of development through which the scientist passed into the seer;

and it may be said that he found his life-work in preparing the material for such a study, in demonstrating and illustrating the theory of correspondence, and in striving to widen the accepted view of the occurrence and scope of divine inspiration. Those who read the original Prospectus of the Swedenborgian Association can scarcely miss the hand of its Secretary in it. How much Wilkinson expected from the new body appears in the following letter [1] :—

" The Laws of the latter (the Association) are just completed and by the next steamer I hope to send you a copy of them ; when, if you decidedly approve, we shall look to have what support you can fairly award us. That much may be done now, and in the way of a New Method in Knowledge, I, for one, have not the slightest doubt. It seems to me that when a state perishes, through a decadent process, there is, at the end, a reversion to the principles of such a state (a ' fleeing to the mountains ') and an appropriation of them in the new principles of a new state. Besides, such principles are used at that time for the purposes of justice and judgment ; they are the marks from which the departure dates, the measures of its length, and the judges of its pretexts. Now in this way, as it seems to me that the Scientific state is actually consummated, must we not refer back to the Works of the presumed Father of Inductive Science, viz., ' the great Lord

[1] Letter to Mr Henry James, March 3, 1845.

Bacon,' and see what can he got out of him for our
purposes ; in what light his genius will acknowledge
his modern children, and a few such points ?   I
propose therefore studying his Works with a view to
this scheme of proceeding, and endeavouring to
measure the moderns by him and him by Swedenborg.
Probably I can achieve no more than a few suggestions put boldly forward, which, however, would be
enough to excite thought and to jog people out of
some of their ruts.   It is manifest that we want a
Novum Organon Scientiarum, and I have an increasing
confidence that the germs which will evolve it are
all contained in Swedenborg's Theological Writings,
and this in the very simplest, or highest, form."

Wilkinson's use of terms was not unfrequently
arbitrary ; it appears that here he anticipates that the
Association was to fulfil some age of Science by its
publications.   The result does not appear to have
followed, for Bacon was not brought in as judge.
Swedenborg's earlier writings show him fully abreast
of Science so far as it existed in his day, and his
speculative vigour is beyond question.   His follower
was inclined to regard him as prophetic in this regard
also, and to read into Science some internal meaning
from Swedenborg.   Certainly a " clearing house "
of the sciences, an assistance in the correlation of
scientific discovery, is a *desideratum* recognized
more generally than it was sixty years ago, but still
far from attainment.

But it must be confessed that there are occasions upon which it is difficult to " localize " Wilkinson accurately. Such an occasion is seized upon by Mr Henry James in the letter from which the following extract is taken. The letter illustrates the true friendship between the two men, the faithfulness and outspoken criticism of the writer, the implied tolerance of that criticism on the part of the receiver. Mr James is acknowledging a copy of " The Human Body in its Connexion with Man," a book which Wilkinson had dedicated to him.[1]

" I have read the great book, you may be sure with eyes enormously expanded, and mouth in sympathy. Such a tremendous volley of strength and brilliancy lifting my name into the astonished air ! The reaction was instantaneous. I said to my wife, ' This is sport to Wilkinson, no doubt ; for great men like to show their magnanimity by condescension to small ones ; but it is death to me. I shall buy a small place in some sheltered nook of the Hudson River, and never let my unworthy head be seen in the city. Such an honour put upon one binds him to keep the peace evermore. Farewell henceforth all my intellectual activities, all my lectures, newspaper squibs and all ! ' But the tumult is now subsiding, and I am able to read the post-dedicatory portion of the volume with attention.

" All your part of the book is absolutely marvellous-

[1] Letter from Mr Henry James, September 9, 1851.

I find all readers to agree in this. They say that you exhaust human power in the direction of rhetoric, and that there is no use of looking for fine writing after this. Your thought is so organic, you think so concretely, that one feels, when in intellectual converse with you, as if he were struggling in the folds of huge icthyosauri, or dancing a jig with gleesome megatheria. It would be a monstrous compliment to the world at large to say that you were ever going to be a popular writer. Scholars will rejoice in you as in abundance of hid treasure, but only in a better world than this will you become known to the multitude. And there seems a just Providence in this. If you were well recognized, at your worth as a writer, you would so dwarf all our existing celebrities as to have the whole field of literature to yourself, and extinguish every publisher but him who put forth your book. You will have, you *must* have inevitably, a great fame; but it will be ratified only by the very best voices of the race. I see the book is advertised to be reprinted by a Philadelphia house, the head of which, Mr Welford tells me, is in London at present, and I presume therefore in communication with you. The advertisements may, however, be merely a *feeler* of the public pulse.

" The matter of the book, too, is glorious, for the most part. The whole truth of it, as exhibiting the loving co-partners of spirit and matter, is beyond price, and the suggestiveness of every page accordingly is unequalled in my experience. But I confess to some disappointment too, owing probably (nay, I am sure), to my own dulness. That is, I do not see precisely to what practical end you would make all this correspondential lore avail. I know well enough when I read Swedenborg, what the bearing of all his disclosures in relation to correspondence, is. I know that they all tend to the glorification of the Lord, or divine natural man. But I do not find myself in as full or flowing sympathy with you. Then again I am additionally bothered every little while with sinewy strokes of orthodoxy, which would delight John Calvin : not that good orthodoxy which seizes firmly the Kernel of the truth and throws away the shell, but apparently a sort that insists upon the shell as equivalent to the kernel. I am sure, I repeat, that I do not understand you, and I will wait therefore for subsequent readings to sharpen my wit. But, for the present, it appears to me from the face of your book either that you have some knowledge which you do not impart to other men in relation to the Christ, or else that you differ *toto cœlo* from Swedenborg concerning Him. You employ habitually such remarkably Calvinistic language about the Christ—and it often seems so consciously and *wilfully* introduced—that I am dumbfounded, and expect to hear the bones of good old Swedenborg rattle with indignation. The mischief of the old Church Christianity is, he says, that they conceive of the Lord only as a Person, or that they have no conception of the divine humanity, but from person, which conception is fatal to the spiritual understanding of the scriptures. I fully abide by this confession. Now you, as it strikes me, delight in mystifying the simple disciple of Swedenborg, and heaping all kinds of tacit contempt upon those principles of biblical interpretation which guided him in denying the divinity of the letter. I have no doubt, all the while, that you have a certain justification in your own knowledge ; but, having it, hang it, why don't you let common people know what it is ? I am unfeignedly mystified by every word you utter on the subject of Christianity. And yet your utterances are so extremely pronounced, and portentous of concealed will, that I dare not treat them as I would those of a feeble man, and dismiss them from all regard. I want to know your philosophic standpoint, the source whence you derive such unprecedented and (an illegible word) theologic *aplomb*. For heaven's sake, therefore, tell me, or (better than this) tell the public, in some brief review of a book or what not, how you understand the *science* of the Christ."

Mr James appears here to lay his finger upon a weak point in his friend's method of work, upon something akin to what we have, in earlier pages, characterized as "impatience." Writing of the deepest subjects from a point of view between that of the theologian and the philosopher, it was incumbent upon Wilkinson, if he would carry his reader with him, to establish his position constantly by careful definition of the terms which he employed. "The light dove, piercing in her easy flight the air, and perceiving its resistance, imagines that flight would be easier still in empty space. It was thus that Plato left the world of sense, as opposing so many hinderances to our understanding. He did not perceive that he was making no progress by these endeavours, because he had no resistance as a fulcrum on which to rest or to apply his powers, in order to cause the understanding to advance. It is indeed a very common fate of human reason first of all to finish its speculative edifice as soon as possible, and then only to inquire whether the foundation be sure."[1] We may acquit Wilkinson of want of industry, as we may acquit him of want of conscience: but his impatience to be in the thick of his work not seldom made his progress from ill-defined premises to the loftiest conclusions unconvincing because logically unscientific. The reader shares the writer's joy in ampler ethers and more divine airs, but fails to join him there, because the initial stages of the climb took place in a fog, as though the early steps, though sufficient

[1] Kant: Introduction to the "Critique of Pure Reason," p. 4.

for the thinker and writer, were not cut deep
enough to guide and support his follower, the
reader.

From time to time, Wilkinson was dissatisfied with
the tendencies taken on by the movement in which
he associated, as the earnest individualist in every
movement is sure to be.[1]

" We take in the *New Era* and are exceedingly
diverted and edified by it. . . . There is in it not
only faith but life, which latter element the New
Church movement now lacks entirely. It is not
that there is not all the Truth in Swedenborg that
we ever contended for, but in his followers it is
unprogressive and destitute of hope and charity,
and therefore their state is liable to be superseded
by any real manifestation, however low, which goes
to the Tables and hearts of the people. I find, in
fact that the old spirit of learning, its exclusiveness
and cruel Latinization, rules just now in Theologicals
and Spirituals; for the philosophers, parsons and
atheists will have it that nothing low shall enter into
the category of Revelation, and that Revelation shall
not go to the low; whereas all the meaning of
Revelation is something told in their own way to
people who cannot understand things otherwise.
Consequently, Revelation is a perpetual descent;
and, until it has come to the million, and Smith
Thomson, Noakes & Co. have each a private reveal-

[1] Letter to Mr Henry James, May 19, 1853.

ment in addition to the public Gospel, the scope of Revelation cannot be complete."

There were, too, doctrinal difficulties, the less easy to be borne because they existed between friends. The letter in which the following long extract occurs was evidently an answer to one in which Mr James pointed out discrepancies between the views of Wilkinson and his friend Mr Augustus Tulk, M.P., as expressed in the work of the latter.[1]

" I forwarded your letter to Mr Tulk as soon as it arrived, since which I have seen him two or three times, and noticed his satisfaction at the correspondence thus begun. You have certainly given me a hard thrust or two, in order to rouse me to show fight, but I am too old a bull in that arena to be provoked in this matter to a ' ferocious rejoinder.' As for a " leisurely rejoinder," which you also desire by your lancinating attack to produce, it shows that, like a Queen of Spain, you desire a prolonged spectacle of my agonies. But I cannot gratify you in this either.

" My present course of work and study is so alien to the subject, that I candidly confess I cannot bring my mind to treat it in that order which you require. Furthermore, to my own conceit at least, I have actually gone *through* it ; and though I can make it, to a certain extent, a matter of recollection, I cannot make it a matter of thought. There is

[1] Letter to Mr Henry James, September 2, 1845.

nothing in it which excites me to activity, nothing
but is as well comprehended when the intellect is
asleep as (when it is) awake. When I catch myself
in any part of its mill-horse round, I say to myself,
like the London vulgar boys, ' There you are at
your old *rigs* again ' : and then I bridle up in a
moment, and perhaps blush slightly to think that
I consumed two mortal years in such occupation.
And when dear Mr Tulk (for whom I have a sincere
respect) is at his gravest, I am unable to look at him,
for fear my slippery mouth should fail me (*se dif-
funderet*), and I should give way to enormous
laughter : so I am debarred of his direct presence,
and eat my handkerchief obliquely. It is impossible
to convert such a state into ' ferocity.' You see
what you ask when you require a leisurely rejoinder ? "

" But, as I should vex you if I left matters thus,
I will go a little into my own history as connected
with Mr Tulk's views. When I first began to read
Swedenborg, it gave a new impetus to my whole
mind, and made me desire to inform myself upon
many subjects and many authors of whom I had
never thought before. And, among other things,
I fell into the very natural idea that there was a
certain parallelism between various books of metaphysics and the writings of Swedenborg, and that
I ought to know something about the former in order
to appreciate our Author correctly. Then I had
no sooner entered the pale of ' the readers ' than

I found a number of eddies of controversy, all blowing away without any prospect of a calm. These circumstances together led two or three of us into rationating about the existence of matter and a number of other such mistaken questions. We bought Berkley, and, finding how dexterous he was, and (above all) that those who objected to him did not understand him (though they were substantially right, for all that, and perhaps were right for not understanding), we thought we had got a pearl of great price and were a chosen few, for whom alone the veil of Isis was about to be uplifted. About this time we came across Mr Tulk's little Book, and now our satisfaction was at its height. As I was the most enthusiastic Berkleyan of the lot, I applied to Mr Tulk for a number of his Books, and by this means made his acquaintance. Great as was my wonderment at Swedenborg, it seemed to me that Mr Tulk's views alone conducted me into the sweetest recesses of the New Church writings, and I spent weeks and months and years in lingering around these fancied spots. It is true that I sometimes had a hard battle to assure myself that they were truths and not potent conjurations; but the will to be comfortable and their pleasant imagery were persistent enough to maintain me in this state for a long time. During this time, I read through the 'Arcana Cœlestia,' and seized upon all the passages I could find confirmatory of my then views; these,

however, were few, far between and so far unsatisfactory that even the best of them required induction
and interpretation in order to make them give the
desired evidence, without a good deal of law-giving
skill, they would easily have been witnesses on the
other side. This was awkward, and it sometimes
struck me that it was not honest to gather strength
in this way. On the other hand, the passages clean
against Tulkism were tens of thousands, but this
cloud of witnesses was modestly put out of court,
under the pretext that their utterances were for the
sensually minded, while on the other hand, the
former class of passages contained direct statements
of principles, and were to govern all the rest. Had
I had the misfortune to be the inventor of the scheme,
probably my *amour propre* and my love of offspring
might have carried me through even the rude shock
of facts like these; but anything short of parental
love *must* break down under such circumstances.
A brat so misbegotten, and manifesting this so fearfully by his contrariety to all honest opinion, might
soon expect to be left by his mere friends, although
his Mother should still cling to him. I began, therefore, instinctively to loosen myself from these views,
prompted thereto by a secret consciousness that
they and Swedenborg were irreconcilable.

" About this time it might be that I strongly felt
that if the Tulkish doctrines were true, God was
still unrevealed, and not the less so because a

sensation of Him once was extant in the world, and His image was in the human mind at the present day. For, if the sensation and the image came by transflux through man, and therefore were mere representatives, I then had the horrifying contradiction of a purely passive or puppet god, of which heaven, hell and man managed the strings and pulled the wires. To such a god I could not pray, for he was, in the very worst sense, the work of men's hands. It would have been spiritual idolatry of the lowest kind, that is, the deification and worship of self ; a thing which heathenism only symbolized, but which, with such a god and such a doctrine, would have been converted into a fact. I left Tulkism upon this point, and acceded to the Scripture declaration that the Lord is the First and the *Last*, and to Swedenborg's doctrine that He is present to man both mediately and *immediately*, and that He alone is Heaven.

" But, although I had thus got rid of this peculiar form of Socinianism, the Berkleyan doctrine still adhered to me, and perhaps I have some remnants of it in my mind even now. I regard it as a logical circle of which the falsity is most easily demonstrated by the fact of impotence. It is evidently out of the order of nature, because it is a thing which can do nothing, and can generate nothing, and therefore has no right to exist. It is precisely like our selfhood in this ; and, what is curious, it makes us doubtful of the existence of each other, and isolates us hopelessly, proving here again where it comes from. Whether or not it is worse than materialism were a piece of casuistry hard to determine. I believe a set of Berkeleyans would be lazier dogs than the same number of materialists ; perhaps as Hindoo Atheists compared with French ones.

" But I was not satisfied to get rid of Berkeley simply on the ground of fruitlessness ; but, by investigating some of his leading aphorisms in the light of the New Church Doctrine, I found I had abundant reason to refuse to start with him through his Logic. His whole book rests, I think, upon the answer which he makes *Philonous* give to the question, ' Can anything but a sensation be like a sensation ? ' and to which answer poor silly *Hylas* of course assents. I do not, and the Book, therefore, with me, stops there ; or, like a burst bubble, goes into an incredibly small compass. Consider here these truths—Man is not Life, but a recipient of Life. The Lord alone is Life, etc., etc., etc.

" Having got so far, by the merciful course of Providence I was led to study Swedenborg's Scientific Works, and, by this means, I furnished the lower storeys of my mind with positive doctrines of nature, in the room of that flatulent stuff which I had once considered to be a just account of the Creation. Thus also I saw the stages through which Swedenborg's mind was empowered from on high to arrive

N

at those doctrines which are given in his Theology, and were as far as possible removed from all we call metaphysics. I saw that to palm Tulkism upon Swedenborg would be to violate his whole mind and education, just as much as to violate the Doctrines of the New Jerusalem. I saw also the reason why the followers of Swedenborg were not so well able to repel attacks and see through trivial difficulties as they ought to be; viz., that they did not train their minds from the beginning to follow the flexible order displayed by God in nature. And this too is the reason why there is a want of greenness and outward beauty in their writings, because they must be comparatively sandy and barren until, in all ways, they can come out into ultimate power and works, which cannot take place until nature in her lowest sphere (*i.e.* in the sphere of mechanics) is seen to be a correspondence of the Lord and the Spiritual World.

" Now I have proceeded historically as regards my own mind, to show you just what I have gone through, and, if there is anything set down egotistically, pray lay it to the account of the method thus chosen, and not altogether to conceit.

" The sum of my belief respecting our friend, Mr Tulk's doctrines, is this: 1. that his view respecting the Lord is Socinianism, so far as this, that it teaches an unrevealed and necessarily unrevealable God, unhinging the worship of Jesus

Christ, by making Him a mere image projected through finite minds. 2. That his sole (intellectual) attachment to Swedenborg is by means of the doctrine of correspondence; which, however, he manages to hold in a fanciful way, unwarranted by his Author, in order to suit his first and last doctrines, viz. Socinianism and Berkeleyism. 3. That his Berkeleyism, a doctrine of nature, instead of being a foundation to his scheme, is but a light outer dross, whereby the natural world is made to smile a little upon the fantasies which his Socinianism produces; and yet that he has no other foundation,—no scientific pillars deep sunken in the nature of mundane things, —and hence is in perpetual insecurity, and can never hope to have half a dozen followers at once. . . .

" On re-reading this, I find I have omitted one subject, which is that, to my apprehension, the Doctrines of the New Church shine with tenfold lustre, and their rationality is tenfold more conspicuous to me since I got rid of the Tulkian method of interpreting them. Only take them as a Revelation, and proceed by a large *Induction from the whole* to read them aright, rather than by logical processes to insinuate your own old ideas into them, and you will see that they are a living fountain of beauty and reason."

Whatever may be thought of the mental process by which Wilkinson rid himself of Berkeleyism and its dependent Tulkism, this letter has importance as a fragmentary spiritual autobiography; and it illustrates once more, if further illustration were necessary, how, for him at least, Swedenborg's writings were upon all questions the ultimate court of appeal, the *ne plus ultra* of arbitration.

We have seen, in the Biographical chapter, that party spirit ran high in the Swedenborgian bodies. Though based actually in profound differences of opinion, it sometimes found occasion for its exhibition in matters of minor importance. Such occasions were, in the bachelors' days when they lived together at Store Street, not unwelcome to Garth Wilkinson and his brother.

There was, however, at least one controversy which cannot be ranked as of minor importance, the editing of Swedenborg's "Diarium" by the Swedenborg Society. It has been alluded to above (page 169) in Wilkinson's letter to Dr Tafel concerning the publication of "The Dreams." Wilkinson gave an account of his first introduction to the MS. in a letter to his *fiancée*.

"Yesterday [1] evening Mr Elwell came to see me, as did also Mr A. Wornum. We all three went together in the evening to Mr Sibly's to see the original manuscript of Swedenborg's Diary. It is literally immense: so closely written, and withal so illegible from abbreviations that it will be a work of great labour to edit it. At the same time the

[1] July 24, 1839.

contents are highly curious, and I am quite anxious to see it printed. The whole will fill 8 or 9 octavo volumes. There are particulars about numbers of the persons of antiquity, and also about many illustrious moderns. Altogether it is a most wonderful book."

More than a half century later, when few of those who had discussed an almost forgotten matter can have been living, he wrote to a friend :—

" I [1] cannot separate between Swedenborg's 'Diarium' and his published writings, or think that the jottings of the former are any more mere dreams or visions than his memorable Relations in his published Works. . . . But for my persistent and insistent action, the 'Diarium' would never have been published by the Swedenborg Society when it was. It was a dead letter in MS. in the hands of the Rev. Mansah Sibley, who resisted its then publication. I think that the Rev. M. Sibley died in the nick of time, and so the Swedenborgian Society got hold of the MS. It belonged really to the Royal Academy of Sciences of Stockholm, having been borrowed from it, and not returned. Through Baron Berzelius, I got leave from the Academy for its publication, and personally sent the MS. off to Professor Immanuel Tafel at Tübingen. At that time it was said by a New Church Minister that if the 'Diarium' was published it would 'disband the Church.' I persevered, notwithstanding."

[1] Letter to Mr J. Thomson, October 7, 1894.

Wilkinson was strong enough to carry his point and to crush opposition in this matter; but the feeling of opposition remained and showed itself in disapproval and resentment.

But the continuous and heavy tasks of translation in which he soon engaged himself deprived the elder brother alike of time and inclination for unnecessary controversy. The strength of his opinions tended rather to isolation than to debate; and he did not without need appear in public Swedenborgian matters. Indeed, even before his practice absorbed him for a long series of years, he relied almost entirely upon the written, as distinguished from the spoken, word for the promulgation of what he believed and thought.

In 1847 and 1849 Wilkinson delivered lectures before the Swedenborg Association. The extract which follows is an answer to criticism upon the latter.[1]

" Your onslaught number two is more serious. You cite from me that ' there is less of the Divine seed in the world than there was in Swedenborg's mind a hundred years ago, and, if we go on at this rate, there will soon be none left.' Now read the context and remember the occasion. Remember that I was speaking to nobody but the Swedenborg Association, which professes to carry out Swedenborg's doctrines through all things. The passage

[1] Letter to Mr Henry James, June 28, 1849.

never was meant to convey anything but a rebuke to *that audience* for having done nothing, for having possessed themselves of Swedenborg and never sown, reaped, or resown him. It was perfectly true of *them*. They have so put themselves under Swedenborg, that if they don't follow *him* out, they do nothing. Had I not been (very unwillingly) addressing that body, I should never have mentioned Swedenborg's name, should hardly have thought of him. Of the very people there present, I believe every one to live in an atmosphere and stratum of truths deeper and wider than Swedenborg ever dreamt of : only not consciously, because they see only Swedenborgically. I believe that our modern plane of existence is human and social in quite a new sense, and that good Swedenborg knew not of it. He was not aware of the existence of the Social World, save as an atmosphere : he saw clean through it, and consequently saw nothing in it."

People do not like to be scolded, however faithful and well-intentioned the scolder; and these people revenged themselves upon the scolder by doubting the orthodoxy of his view concerning Swedenborg. The attitude of suspicion taken up by the sectarian class of Swedenborgians was long maintained, and it betrayed itself in a half-hearted support of their champion, in failure to welcome and use his work.

Such an attitude was by no means universal among the Swedenborgians : Wilkinson had always his enthusiastic followers who saw the man and his work as faithful and as of vital importance to their cause. But the doubt and suspicion were evident enough to the subject of them.[1]

" No news has come from Mr Clapp yet, and I am therefore uncertain whether my second batch of proofs has arrived, and whether my Life of Swedenborg is published (in America) or not. Newberry tells me that the New Church people are very decided in their vituperation of the Book, and that they patronize it not at all. He has not sold 200 copies, and will be sadly out of pocket, poor man. However, it is eagerly read by many of those persons whose ear I have desired, and specially by the most intelligent among the Unitarians. I am somewhat curious to know what its fate may be on your side of the water."

The Swedenborgians may have held aloof from the book for a time ; but they ultimately discovered that its aim was good and that it fulfilled its aim. It ran out of print, and a call for a second edition was met in 1888. It remains the classical work upon the subject, alike for the Swedenborgian and the general reader.

Good work is seldom done without opposition and misunderstanding, and there is no need to enter at greater length into old differences of opinion and action than is necessary to show that in his

[1] Letter to Mr Henry James, January 25, 1850.

following of Swedenborg, as in every cause which he espoused, Wilkinson was prepared to stand, and did stand, alone. This was often disheartening. But he had the satisfaction of knowing that opinion came round to his side. Many years before he ended together his writing and his life, he was generally recognized as the most learned, industrious, and outspoken of all who " read the Writings."

Among the various definitions of genius which have been offered, the best known and almost the worst in quality is that which calls it " the transcendent capacity for taking pains." Upon such a definition, and upon much better grounds, Wilkinson's claim to genius as a translator would be unimpeachable.[1]

" ' The Economy of the Animal Kingdom ' is proceeding apace through the press, 208 pages being now printed. This Work does not diminish my interest in the natural philosophy promulgated by Swedenborg. It is, however, a very difficult Treatise to follow ; and, when I tell you that, after reading every proof four times, I still find that I have not half exhausted the meaning, and in many cases have not perceived the ratio of the general order at all, you will, I think, consider that the work is not calculated at first hand for the popular amusement. Deeply interesting as the matter, for the most part, is, the method is perhaps to the full as

[1] Letter to Mr Henry James, February 1844.

instructive to the mind as the matter. There is, every now and then, such a masterly flinging on one side of the obtrusive yet non-essential parts of a subject, and such a long discernment of the quiet, retiring centres and pivots of things. We see a mind for which the still small voices of creation are excellent music, a mind whose stillness is itself so profound that the mixed harmonies are its veriest language. This must incite us all to cultivate a finer sense, and to receive it as a settled truth that there is ever something more in nature than the order first presented to the senses ; that this order is the lowest, a chaos (as it were) of essentials and non-essentials ; and that the latter must be rejected to the sides of the circumference, to give breadth to the series, while the former must be placed in the direct line of descent, and then contemplated as the main progressions of Creative Wisdom. But I must stow this, for I am getting into a Treatise."

More than two years later he is able to write :— [1]

"My labours on the 'Economy' are, I may say, done. The last sheet of my Preface (it makes more than five sheets) is printed ; and, by the next boat, I intend to send you three or four copies of it. I am sure that it is not in *your* way, being altogether critical, literary, biographical, controversial, British-Museum-ish ; and not universal, spiritual, or organic. For I know my own powers, and that they limit me

[1] Letter to Mr Henry James, April 18, 1846.

absolutely to the former walk, and therefore I go in it cheerfully, hoping that it may be of use for better things. To me, everything which dissipates any bit of misconception or nonsense about Swedenborg, or which gives a new correct notion, is of importance ; and my labours are a jotting down of some such things as these. Bibliography, in an extended sense, is the whole idea of them. If they fail of this, they are good for nothing; in so far as they succeed in this, *my* end is realized in them."

The piece of work thus estimated by its author is one of those concerning which Mr Emerson wrote :—

" The admirable preliminary discourses with which Mr Wilkinson has enriched these volume. throw all the contemporary philosophy of England into shade." But it is good to be humble. The spade-work and drudgery which produced these translations and introductions built the foundations of that deep knowledge of Swedenborg's Works which were to bear superstructures valuable to all time to the New Church.

Concerning his translation of Swedenborg's work, " The Generative Organs considered anatomically, physically, and philosophically," Wilkinson wrote :—[1]

" I am bringing out, parallel with my work on the Body, a Translation of Swedenborg's work on the Generative organs of both sexes: a book of singular suggestiveness, though not very com-

[1] Letter to Mr Henry James, August 2, 1850.

patible with the smugness and straightlacedness of many of the followers of Swedenborg. However, the Swedenborg Association has had the boldness to commission me to execute a version. I cannot help regarding it as one small help on the way to a greater liberty of thought and knowledge on sexual subjects. It will at all events make them matters of contemplation, and begin, therefore, to rescue them from that heavily covered animality and hypocrisy which at present lies in them. Our existing education on this head can only be characterized as unconsciously piggish! But when the wings of Science and Spirit come and annex themselves, the gross parts will be raised into the air, and things before invisible and unutterable will be seen to be as clean as the flowers of the field or as the pleasant butterflies, which are the flowers of flowers. But, doubtless, even these must be fenced round, lest the pigs should run grunting to eat them."

This view, that daylight and fresh air will purge the uncleanness which has attached itself to Nature, was quite characteristic of the man. Here, as on the question of publishing Swedenborg's "Diary," he was all in favour of outspeaking.

Wilkinson frequently brought Swedenborg and his message before those in whom he hoped that acquaintance would fructify into service : among such were Thomas Carlyle and Miss Harriet Martineau.[1]

[1] Letter to Miss Marsh, October 22, 1839.

" On Saturday I wrote Mr Carlyle a reply to his kind letter, sending him, on loan, what biographical notices of Swedenborg I could procure. I also gave him a few particulars about the Philosophical Works and the ' Diary of Memorabilia,' which is in manuscript, and I told him my motives for having troubled him so much with the Books, namely, that I wished him to have before him materials for forming and expressing to the world an opinion on the subject. Whether this may produce anything further I know not, and, indeed, having now done my part, I must leave him to himeslf."

Miss Martineau acknowledged his present very sympathetically (October 22, 1838) :—

" It is my intention to read with seriousness and diligence the book you have sent me : and I believe I shall sit down to the work under somewhat less than the ordinary degree of prejudice on the subject. I agree largely in some of the practical parts of the faith of your Church, and thence have a respect by anticipation for the speculative portions which I do not yet understand or agree with. Mr Sampson Reed has been kind enough to furnish me with much material for inight into the belief and practice of your Church, and the more I learn the more desirous I am that both should be better understood than they are."

Of much later date, though brought about by similar propagandist work on Wilkinson's part, are the letters from Robert Browning and Coventry Patmore, both of whom were his old friends.[1]

" MY DEAR DR WILKINSON, — Your kind note did indeed render active—rather than waken— many memories, pleasant and painful together, as must happen in such a case : *you*, however, stay associated with nothing that is other than pleasurable. Thank you very much for the book I shall read with great interest. I well remember the letter in which you recommended me to study Swedenborg. I believe that you and I have always been in accordance as to aspiration and sympathy, though we may differ in our appreciation of the relative importance of facts connected with them.

" I am glad to suppose, both from what you tell me and what you are silent about, that on the whole things go well with you. So may they continue ! I too have an elderly child—a son, and I live with my sister, whom you must have seen in old days when poor Dow was young.

" Believe me, with reiterated thanks for your gift and kind words,—Yours very cordially,

" ROBERT BROWNING."

Mr Coventry Patmore was inclined to regard Swedenborg in the rather odd aspect of a Papist *manqué*. Writing in 1891, he says :—

---

[1] Letter from Mr Browning, May 17, 1887.

" I am very glad to see your handwriting again, after so many years. Your ' cloth differs ' less than you suppose from mine. I claim Swedenborg as the greatest of *Roman* Catholic prophets, since St Augustine at least. Swedenborg's great inspiration, like that of all the Prophets and Apostles, was purely ethical and psychological, and did not prevent him making mistakes about other things, any more than the inspirations of the Evangelists prevented them from giving four different versions of the inscription on the Cross. All the time that S. was abusing the Catholics for holding false doctrine, he was mainly teaching pure Catholic doctrine, as it is and always has been held by the Saints, though the Parish Priest, partly from his own usual ignorance and partly from the brutish condition of his congregation, is compelled to—

> ' Make Truth look as near a lie
> As can comport with her divinity.'

Your own people, you know, are just as stupid, and know no more of what Swedenborg meant than ours do of the meaning of the Breviary. It was Swedenborg mainly that brought me into the Catholic Church."

A year later, Mr Patmore wrote to the same purpose :—

" I am reading your new book with the greatest pleasure and profit, as, indeed, I read all your books.

The 'Summa' of St Thomas Aquinas and your volume of selections from Swedenborg have, for many years, formed the *groundwork* of all my reading : and, you will perhaps be surprised to hear that they seem to me to be but two aspects of one and the same Catholic truth, St Thomas appealing mainly to the ear of rational faith, Swedenborg to the perceptive faculty."

Swedenborg's writings have been indicted as teaching an intellectual, rather than a spiritual, religion—a religion more of the head than of the heart; and the indictment is supported by the inscription which he saw, in one of his visions, upon a Temple in Heaven, *Nunc licet intrare intellectualiter in mysteriâ fidei.* Wilkinson's work, concerned largely with the intellectual apprehension of matters spiritual, might seem open to a similar charge : but, in fact, he would have none of a religion which, while it flattered the mind, left the conduct untouched.[1]

" Really and truly, the worshipping of this idol intelligence is the greatest absurdity that can be, as it is the prevailing one of the present day. It is but a shade higher than Mammon-worship. For, only think what intelligence *is*, apart from use. What does it do ?   What monuments does it leave ? What men does it lead to Heaven ? "   He goes on to distinguish between knowledge and wisdom,

---

[1] Letter to Miss Marsh, December 3, 1839.

and to extol a religion which seeks the latter. In another letter of the same year, he returns to the subject from a slightly different point of view.

" I am very much pleased with the mention you make of Sampson Reed's book. I was confident you would like it, and I am quite of your opinion regarding the bearing of the sentence you quote from Carlyle. After all, it seems to me to come to this, that man sees not only with his eye, but with *himself*, and consequently his vision is such as his interior being is. This is clearly implied in the commonest way of stating it, when we say, ' He sees,' for, to see well not only implies a clear *cornea* but a fit ground of vision. It is not the mere transparency of the intellect which makes the mind's sight acute and perfect, but the will also must have a predisposition to be affected with the things which the intellect perceives. All (of) which our friend Sampson has stated far better than I can do, yet still it sometimes makes an impression and even sets the thing in a better light when those we love talk it over in their own familiar way, and that for the very reason just given; that then the will is sure to be somewhat fixed upon the same point as the intellect."

And, in fact as well as in theory, Wilkinson kept a just distance between faith and knowledge, holding, with Bishop Pearson, that " those things which

o

are apparent are not said properly to be believed but to be known." [1]

" I have read your strictures on Mr Tennant (See page 74) with interest. First, the facts are important, and I do believe them to be facts. As to the theory of God's intervention, let us hold it very gently. However, that God does intervene in the most partial as well as in the most universal ways who can doubt? Furthermore, that there are certain hieroglyphical or correspondential powers given to certain actions—that gesture and attitude bring spirit with them—I hold to be indisputable. If we could work the Science of correspondences, we should be enabled to perform many wonders, without any new substances being called into play. In Mesmerism, if we knew what wrinkle of face and what play of fingers gave the shape correspondent to any drug, we might produce its effects upon a susceptible patient by one look or one pointing or one beckon. This is a deep part of the universal laws of nature. The Name of God has also, I doubt not, its own *natural* powers."

As his writings gained acceptance and as he became himself acknowledged as the most extensive existing repository of Swedenborgian lore, Wilkinson's correspondence became enormous, it must have constituted a severe tax upon his leisure; but he

[1] Letter to Mr Henry James, June 1, 1849.

never complained, and it may be doubted whether any inquirer failed to receive an answer. Many such correspondents wrote from America. One inquires about Jasper Svedborg, the father of Emanuel Swedenborg, another writes to suggest that a new edition of " The Human Body " should be prepared, with anatomical plates for the benefit of lay students; there are inquirers concerning the correspondential bearings of commerce, the early African nations and upon a host of other like matters.

From answers to such correspondents and also from *obiter dicta* on Swedenborgian subjects, I propose to give extracts, allowing them to stand disjointed, as they came day by day from his pen. They will be found loosely grouped together according to their subject matter.

[1] " ' *Fairbrass* ' [2] is not indeed, as you well remark, devoted to ' the light and pretty ' and new ideas and connexions of the narrative with the birds and flowers. All nature is always conversing about good and evil, and nothing of her inner voices, irrespective of these grand and terrible Rulers, is light or pretty in her. The Science of Correspondence talks : ' Day unto day uttereth speech, and night into night showeth knowledge.' There is no speech or language when their voice is not heard.

[1] Letter to Mr John Martin, October I, 1894.
[2] A character in " A Child's Story," by E. Pemberton.

Their line (?) is gone out into all the earth, and their words unto the end of the world. In them hath He set a Tabernacle for the Sun."

" Since, without these spiritual factors, there is no truth in talking walking-sticks or kneeling knights, inventions about them otherwise inspired are frivolous, and do not touch anything of the heart, *even in children*. It is the shining down from an internal light upon a dark world that gives zest to all myth and fairyland."

[1] " I shall most likely stroll down about 2, when the Procession leaves the Palace, and though myriads of common human beings, *uncrowned*, will most likely be all I shall see, I shall have feelings which are recompense for the sight of Royalty I shall scarcely get. We before talked of our common awe in witnessing the majesty of human masses. I always now think doctrinally of such things as even these. I cannot help looking toward the Being in whom all these particles of Man are in union or oneness, that Divine and unbounded Man of whom all men in all times and countries and planets are but the diverse images and forms; whilst he is their unchanging and Substantial Humanity.

[2] " I should have liked to be one of your party

[1] Letter to Miss Marsh, November 8, 1837. This refers to Queen Victoria's visit to the City on the following day, Lord Mayor's Day.

[2] Letter to Miss Marsh, September 11, 1838.

when you visited the Great Western Steamer. I
do take such a deep interest in all these new births
of this Time, for they seem to me signs of still greater
changes which are passing over the souls of men,
from which they come forth to tell tales to those
who like to listen, of what is going on in the invisible
Kingdom, where they originate."

Spiritual and Natural Nourishment

[1] " Reading 'The Arcana' yesterday, I came on a
passage on Spiritual and Natural nourishment, and
the correspondence between them, and how they
help each other !

' That Scientifics and truths sustain men's souls
is manifest from the desires of knowing instinct
in all men, and likewise from the correspondence
of food with scientifics : which correspondence also
manifests itself during the taking of food, for, if
this be done whilst one is discoursing and listening
to discourse, the vessels which receive the chyle are
opened, and the man is more fully nourished than
if he (or she) eats alone. Spiritual truths and the
instruction in them would have such an effect with
men if they were in the love of good ' ('Arcana,'
n. 6078).

" How important therefore it is not to confirm

[1] Letter to Miss E. L. Pertz, October 29, 1883.

the habit of isolation at what might be sacrament-times, will come home to you."

SIGNIFICANCE OF EARTHQUAKES [1]

" You ask me about Earthquakes, what they proceed from ?   Do you mean naturally or spiritually ?   Spiritually, Swedenborg tells us, they represent and proceed from ' changes of the state of the church ' ; and I should think, from changes of the grander kind.   The Earth represents the natural man ; the Earth's surface, the natural man exteriorly illuminated by the heat and light of the Spiritual Sun ; that is by love and faith ; but if only exteriorly, and not interiorly, his Earth's green and illumined surface consists of the hypocritical pretences of love, and the mere knowledges of faith. The depths of the Earth, from which the Earthquakes begin, represent the interiors of the natural man at variance with the exteriors ; and consequently Earthquakes represent the state when the interiors are about, by mighty commotions, to destroy the fair surface of the exteriors ; or when inward lusts of evil are about to overwhelm everything of spiritual knowledge and even of seeming love, in the superficial aspect of the man ; and to reduce the whole man into a final or homogeneous state of barren, stony desolation."

[1] Letter to Miss Marsh, September 10, 1839.

THE CLOTHING OF ADAM AND EVE [1]

" Tell —— that I *think* there must be survivals of correspondences among savage tribes. The fig-leaves came as a deep perception to the inspired writer of the Word in Genesis. They signify the lapse out of celestial into natural good remaining, into its lower mind, now covering the deeper lost innocence. Adam and Eve made these for themselves (verse 7). But (verse 21) The Lord made them skins ; signifying a deeper lapse, and a greater covering. It is all written in ' Arcana,' vol. i."

MENTAL DEPRESSION, CONSCIOUS SEPARATION FROM GOD [2]

" You mistake greatly, if you think that I have a greater insight in times of trouble, into the uses and ends of temptation, than other people, or than you. Trouble involves the want of this perception, and hence the confused state of mind which all wretchedness causes. All wretchedness consists in the feeling that we are living for no end ; and really, that we are thus living unconnected from the Supreme End, or the Lord. If you take any case of unhappiness whatever, you will find that this is the case ; they all involve the doubt in the man's mind, of ' what good is my life to me ? ' In other

[1] Letter to Miss E. L. Pertz, August 23, 1888.
[2] Letter to Miss Marsh, September 10, 1839.

words, ' what am I living for ? '   And thus they
all consist in a felt separation, greater or lesser,
higher or lower, from the End of Ends.   Thus you
perceive, that in times of trouble, every man alike
must feel a want of perception of the use of the
things which come over him.   Yet still there are
differences in men on this matter.   In some the
whole thing appears perfectly hopeless, for they
have no faith in happiness at all, or in other words,
there is no affirmation of any end in any part or
faculty of their mind or being.   These are they who
delight in being miserable, and are the most selfish
of men, and in almost total separation from the
Supreme Goodness and Love.   They are misan-
thropists, and only admit the existence of God, that
they must have the power of charging Him with
their miseries.   Their miseries are not temptations,
but are the results of the loss of worldly things,
such as power, money or fame.   But there is quite
another class of sufferers, (are we not all sufferers
in one class or the other, or a class intermediate
between the two ?) whose griefs are the results of
the perception of evil in themselves, and whose
trials are all purifying temptations.   They constantly
feel, more and more deeply, that they are not good,
and that thus they are not connected as they should
be with the one great end of Being.   Yet still in
all their gloom they see just enough of star and
moonlight overhead, to show them that there is a

plan of journey, and a series of definite objects to be passed, and a number of ends to be attained; though the light does not suffice them, perhaps, to distinguish definitely a single thing: still less are they cheered by a single warming ray. They only have a cold knowledge of the general fact, without any particulars to illustrate it, and without any comfort in knowing it. But they persevere, for God is with them, turning their darkness into light, and their moon into a sun. They are big with the coming day, and are unceasingly advancing towards it; and every moment of gloom is the necessary way to it, for there is a Divine Force, which is driving itself on through them, and the darkness, and kindling day in the midst of both.

"What can it be, but God, which thus makes us persevere in our way, when we have no *pleasure* in persevering? which gives us a faith in the final good of our being, when we have no view of any good at all? The battle and the victory of temptation, when a man fights against himself, and against his likings is indeed a mystery, which requires us to admit something more than self as the agent of the wondrous conflict. I often feel, that for a man to go forth in helm and plume, and fight against his fellows, is natural and easy enough, for all the motives of *himself* drive him to do so; but that for a man to fight against his pleasures, inclinations, natural propensities, and early acquired habitudes, is no such easy thing to conceive; and indeed it could not be conceived, if it were not felt, more or less in all temptation. ' A man's enemies are those of his own household.' "

MANY INHABITED WORLDS [1]

" I welcome the moral of your muse. Some good flowing in and flowing out is indispensable, to give real worth to song. There must be psalm, whether plain or veiled at the centre, and your dream comes to you from good stars, teaching you that temptation undergone and vanquished, and the cheer that comes after are the Way, the Truth and the Life of whatever is finally lovely.

" You deal accurately with the astronomic conception of the dead moon and the blasted volcanic coffin of it. Can fire have existed there if there were no atmosphere ? My belief is that there is no planet or sufficient satellite but has human beings upon it. Looking from the faith that the creative Love and Wisdom of the Almighty myriads of solar systems cannot satisfy the Infinite Man and Saviour, the revealed thought is welcome, that an unmeasurable variety of Man is demanded to fill the nursery planets of the firmament. Also there is, as in Geology, a perfect order in this immensity. You want flesh and bone of every kind, from the summit

[1] Letter to Miss Alice Head, December 24, 1898.

to the base of the universal Man here discerned. Therefore we have not brains enough or imaginations enough to limit the breath, and consequently spiritual capacity, of the Lunar people. The longer we live, if we are advancing in true light, the more we shall find that truth eclipses fiction, that godly science, in its activity and rejection of materialism and sensualism, and in its capacity for learning and distinction, uses imagination as a torch wherever it is useful, but never disparages the Inner Sun from which all light and heat proceed originally."

[1] " Of course the loss of those nearest and dearest to us has a Providential Use for us, if we are living in the Way, the Truth and the Life. It is fearfully and wonderfully elevating to all who take it aright ; like the first experiences of flight to a young bird, when the Mother commands it to have faith in Wing and Air. Great things follow from the human faith ; among the rest, wings for the mind to explore the Spiritual World to which the beloved have been taken."

[2] " Our loving sympathy is with you in your great sorrow. No consolation can make it other than a crown of sorrows. Such a husband taken from you in the height of his years and powers, and such a life to be filled on your lonely way !

[1] Letter to Mr Tafel on the death of his daughter, Mrs Pertz, September 15, 1893.
[2] Letter to Mrs Tafel on the death of her husband, January 11, 1893.

" With the Lord's help alone you will be equal to it ; and in fulfilling your years you will find the only consolation, until your hour of Victory also comes, and the heavenly marriage is reached.

" His work to our eyes looks broken off, but to Providence this cannot be. He did what he could do, and no other man in the world was equal to the quantity and quality of his achievements for the New Church. In that case he has virtually left nothing undone, and in his own line nothing that wants doing. Others will be raised up to continue on the plains where he left off upon the mountains. And then he is at work above by influx, and will guide the choice of those who will be his successors. Let us feel sure that the Lord's Church will not suffer because one potent spirit more is transferred to the heavenly side of her Armies."

COMMERCE

[1] " Your Mama tells me that —— finds support in Swedenborg for her view that each country should shut out the fruits and produce of all other lands. Almost anything can be confirmed out of a voluminous writer by taking parts and isolating them from the general meaning. Humanity also is a whole, consisting of different and distinct parts or organs. Some of it is family-humanity, some is

[1] Letters to Miss E. L. Pertz, May 30 and June, 1889.

clannish, some in larger governmental blocks, some in great empires, some almost in world-empires. The latter is the case especially with Oceanic England. According to these diversities, communications exist and are limited and extended. In the family scale, at the bottom of ' civilization,' people kill their own sheep, if they have any, and make their own candles, in that case, etc., etc., etc. All these things are profoundly traditional. But none of this is a rule for any other organic Society. The people of the heart, which lives in the widest circula- tion of goods, are not to be measured by the people of the bones, which want to be still. The people of the brains, which live in thought and will, are not to be measured by the limbs, which exist to be governed.

" But enough of this.   Swedenborg's doctrine *here* is that the people of this earth are fundamentally *commercial,* or existing and flourishing in the inter- change of commodities between all countries ; so that each may have what all has. The Reason is, that this Earth belongs to the general skin in the Grand Man ; which skin is the universal covering, everywhere communicating with itself. *And on this function depends the production of the external Word, and the Incarnation itself.* The externality of the mind of this earth made it possible that the Word could be written here in this *end and terminus* of creation ; and that the Lord might be then *communicated in the Spiritual World* to the entire universe. I send you the Book in which you will find this. . . .

" As to commerce, I should like to see any of Mr Mill's papers on his view of the subject. Commerce is as irremovable as human Society on this earth is. So there is no call to defend it. The pillars of *our* mankind rest upon it. But, for the sake of dear individual minds, it is important not to accept fallacies, or to confirm them into falsities, for fallacies dwarf the mind, and falsities pervert it.

" No view against Commerce itself can be reconciled with Christianity. The perversions of it require the acknowledgment of the good of it, and they are to be dominated by the new conscience, and commerce is to be thus regenerated. But, for the rest, it is no worse than the Church and State, Medicine, Law, Trade, Artizanship, and every other department of Life. The *whole* head is sick, and the *whole* heart faint, not commerce alone. All demand the new daily *Duty-doing*.

" If all the dates in Biskra could be the unquestioned property of the poor Arabs and Negroes, the result would be that they would sink under the glut and gluttony of the goods, and next year there would be no Date-palms left. So of every other place and property where non-proprietors came into possession of what is not their own. The thing itself, the property, would cease. The world requires Self-interest to carry it on, until human-love-interest comes. And self-interest, *with its fore-sights*, does not exist in the lowest classes anywhere. As commerce is a divinely permitted necessity for this earth, so no final race here can have its perfect bodily development without a table temperately set out with the fruits and meats of all the climates from the pole to the pole.

" My hand is shaky in my 78th year, but I want to say the truth, that truth may come and be done.

" Finally, I hope you will daily enjoy all the fruits you can, and some of the wines."

DOCTRINE OF SUCCESSIVE REVELATIONS [1]

" I miss writing to you, though, owing now to feeble health, I am deficient in energy, though warm in will. But Christmas reinforces love with an external command. . . .

" There is little for me to record. I am still trying a little work in writing,[2] now an Egyptian theme, perhaps nameable as Egypt Scriptural and Egypt Monumental. As I emerge from my weakness, I look forward to continuing this attempt to introduce a Spirit from the Word into the dead body of Egyptology. The subject may open into interest : for the students of the hieroglyphics and the tombs and temples never think that there is any connexion

[1] Letter to Mr John Thomson, December 22, 1898.
[2] Isis and Osiris, etc.

but a fabulous one between the detailed Biblical Revelation and the so-called history of the Pharaohs. I know you like to hear of my small ventures.

" The demolition of the Dervishes is agreeable to my apprehension. The worst of them have been received into the Spiritual world where there is skill to treat them. The rest will make excellent soldiers and men of duty for the British and Irish Chain, one Day to become golden and impearled round the neck of Africa."

The Doctrine of Successive Revelations [1]

" You told me on Thursday that it was believed among your countrymen in Vej that the gift of singing among them was suggested and imitated from the songs and notes of birds.

" It may interest you to read the following rough translation from the poem ' De Rerum Naturâ ' of Lucretius. ' Imitating the liquid notes of birds by the mouth came long before the time when men were able to chant their slender ditties as songs, and to please the ears. Moreover the sighs of the West Wind, Zephyrus, through the hollows of reeds, first taught these countrymen to blow their hemlock flutes. Then, little by little, they learnt the dulcet means which the pipe pours forth to the play of the fingers of the singer ; the pipe, abundant throughout the pathless groves, and woods and forest slopes,

[1] Letter to Prince Momolu Massaquoi, September 15, 1894.

the solitary places and divine houses of the shepherds " (Book v. 1379-1387).

" The earliest age, the *pre-Adamite*, was not savage, but in " the innocence of ignorance." It had no bad inheritance in it to lame its nature. The men and women had Freewill, and, though designed for elevation to the celestial state called Adam, they could stop if they chose at any earlier state. Some did so stop; and are now probably the Cave-men; so called Aborigines, but of many kinds. However, all were then gifted of human faculties, and at first learnt nothing from birds and from Zephyr.

" In later stages, indeed, man, a different creature, has learnt from outward nature, in fact, learns everything from without. But, in the beginning nature was a correspondential image and shadow of him and from his summit he saw through its veil, and gave their acceptable symbolic names to all living things.

" Lucretius represents the Savage Man, and mistakes him for the primeval man. The best of your race, the African, represent the Remains of the Adamic Race, but not of the Adamic Church, which perished.

" The doctrine of successive Churches or Revelations is thus all-important to the understanding of Swedenborg. These Churches are in a series, one after another, and are " the ways of God to Man." They are what the Greek Testament calls Æons. When they are comprehended in their order, Revelation can become Theology."

P

PANTHEISM

[1] " Are you Channing's critic in the ' Spirit of the Age ? ' Right or wrong, Channing seems to have vibrated back pretty entirely into a respectable Anglo-Saxon Arianism, purged of the very essence of the French socialist. I am not prepared to offer any verdict, except on one point : I must say on that, that it appeals to me that Fourier least of all men deserves the title of a Pantheist.   There are no religious doctrines to be found in him worth notice, and what little he has said theologically I could have wished he had let alone. But then observe the hypothesis upon which he has worked the problems of existence. It is a distinctly Anthropomorphic Hypothesis : a position that God's works can be interpreted by man, because they are like man's works, and interpreted by man's mind because it is like God's mind. All that immensely reaching genius to which the universe lies so coloured and so subject consists in his implicit belief in some axiom of the Manhood of God. It is this which makes him give feeling and quasi-feeling to planets, suns, vegetables and minerals. It is this which causes him to treat the universe as a vast common-sense house, full of utensils for human-like wants and purposes. It is this which enables him, from a new altitude of scornful benevolence, to call down

[1] Letter to Mr Henry James, December 27, 1849.

thunders upon the impenetrability and impossibility which the recent generations have been building up everywhere. It is this which gives him hope, faith, love and science. In short, if he has not made use of a Personal God theologically, he has at least never ceased to employ Him algebraically, as the only cypher which can work the unknown into the known and present us with the universe as a patent quantity at last. Now, God cannot be too present in all thought, and it is a peculiar glory of Fourier that he has introduced Him personally as the x of his vast mathematics : the x itself having all the benefit of a cypher, at the same time that it is itself, by illustration from the human mind, the very plainest of substances. These thoughts flitted through me when I read the well-ordered dispute between Channing and his critic.

" On the other hand, I suspect that our Arians do not themselves hold the Personality so strongly as Fourier did, and that they separate it at a certain altitude from the Humanity, when, it seems to me, the Personality perishes."

Hell's Torments [1]

" I think there is an error in your last about the signification of ' the worm that never dies.' You seem to think that it signifies ' a troubled conscience '

[1] Letter to Miss Marsh, November 13, 1838.

and that the evil in a future life have this troubled
conscience. To me this would, I confess, be a very
unpleasant belief, because I see no reason why a
created being should be kept in a continual state of
self-reproach, without being able to practise self-
amendment. It rather seems to me that the existence of a troubled conscience shews a certain interior
love of the good and horror of the evil. But the
testimony of Swedenborg is quite conclusive on the
point. He asserts that the pains of conscience
form no part of the pains of Hell—for, says he, in the
1st Vol. A. C. those who are there, ' have no con-
sciences.' They have in fact no repentance, no
remorse, no sorrow for sin of any kind whatever.
And the reason is plain, that in their final state
(which thus even to them is a *rest*), the adventitious
goodness or truth, which dwelt in their outer mind
is quite removed and they are nothing but evil and
falsity—nay, Swedenborg says they themselves ' are
evils and falsities.' Now the existence of conscience
of course depends upon the co-existence of two
contrary elements in the soul, but in the other state
the one element is taken away, and the other becomes all-ruling. Let it not however be therefore
supposed that the New Church doctrine diminishes
the terrors of Hell. The real question is, does it
make evil more or less terrible to you and to me
than it was before ; for evil and the false are the
only terribles of Hell. I believe it makes it in-

finitely more so. I should then say that the true torment consists in the loves of evil themselves; for these loves being finite and most selfish burn to be gratified by universal dominion, but being checked and limited necessarily by each other what a source of disappointed misery is here! Self, in its efforts to destroy other *selfs*, which efforts are perpetually resisted, and tend therefore to narrow and compress *itself*—this self is the worm which never dies. It might also be said that each of the cupidities of the natural man is that worm; in each of them there is the desire of universal dominion, and as this cannot be, each is, by its nature, weak and miserable."

CONDITIONS FOR UNDERSTANDING SPIRITUAL PROGRESS [1]

" I think I do recollect once saying that to understand the Arcana C. it was necessary we should have gone through the states therein unfolded: and I cannot help yet thinking it must be so. I do not see how by this remark my Emmy or anyone else is debarred from improvement: for is not our Lord continually leading us through new states of spiritual being, and do we not find ourselves then conscious of truths which were before unknown, which before *could not* be known? for *then* we *had*

[1] Letter to Miss Marsh, October 9, 1838.

not the faculties which discern them : I think it
manifest that if a thing has happened to ourselves
we can far better understand a description of it,
and this is even more applicable in spiritual things,
where each state is quite new, and perhaps quite
unlike all other states and so not to be comprehended
by them.   In fact I might say that each state to
be seen requires a separate eye or faculty of seeing.
And whenever a new state of our being is unfolded
there is more or less self-consciousness of it, which
is its *eye*, and in this self-consciousness, after all, is
contained all the knowledge we have of metaphysics
or philosophy *as realities in ourselves*.   But it so
happens, that no man is conscious of all or even of
a very small part of what is transacted in his interior
man, though no doubt this consciousness will be
greatly increased, and in proportion as men become
more unselfish, they will become *larger selves*.   Now,
the Arcana gives all that can be told in natural
language both of those changes of which we are,
and those of which we *are not* (but may one day) be
conscious, and therefore I think it is pretty clear
that our real knowledge of the internal things of
that book must be gradually produced by the gradual
development and self-consciousness of the internal
man.   It will then be a description of what men are.
Then indeed things, which no patience of hammering
investigation could beat out, will be quite easily
seen and affirmed as true of ourselves—as truths

in ourselves, which are substantial and self-evident only. But, at present the Book describes of the internal man much of which the interior of the men of this dark age are not composed, so that they can have no self-consciousness of it—and their knowledge must be nothing more than the knowledge of certain sayings in a certain book ; of which it may be clearly known what is *said*, but what it *means* in reference to *them*, or in other words, what it *is*, must be quite *unknown*."

THE SPIRITUAL IMPORTANCE OF HUMBLE DUTIES [1]

"Did you read through the first Vol. of the Arc. Coel. ? I am truly glad that you feel such a deep interest in the writings of Swedenborg, and I am sure we shall always find them not only a solid support in all the situations of grave and active life, but also a delightful recreation of the mind and the affections in converse on evenings when worldly care is excluded, and when *other* religions are also generally shut out, in order that they may not hurt the cheerfulness of the occasion ; but it is a peculiarity of ours that it is our rule of conduct *in* the world, our guide *from the world* to the regions of abstract reason, and spiritual beauty, and even the life and soul of liveliness with the lively, provided they be cheerful from a godly, and therefore

[1] Letter to Miss Marsh, September 4, 1837.

truly *human* ground.   May our Lord Jesus be with
us and in us and apply divine truths to the purifica-
tion and ordination of every act of our lives !   I
believe that there is no act, however degraded in its
outward form, which may not contain within it a
Spiritual beauty which is ineffable : because every
deed of man contains his will, and there may be
heavenly motives involved in doing the minutest
thing.   Every act done because it is a duty to God
and His church to do it, is beautiful above language
and conception ; and the real delight of it is that
stream of living waters in which the good live, when
the natural part of them is happily removed forever.
Now, pray, dear Girl, as no principle of philosophy is
worth a pin, which does not illustrate common or
real life in the world, look at the consequences of
this principle as applied to many vile and degraded
trades and callings.   Recollect that nothing can be
done which may not be done from a heavenly motive.
Recollect that if a barber crops the hair in the best
manner *because* it is his duty ; because it is his
religion to do the least thing with all his will, such
man really does an act which contains within it
Love to God and love to his neighbour ; all the
' Law and the Prophets ' are involved in every
such deed, and so it is shown that in this common
and disregarded employ there may be something
really Divine !   'Tis true 'tis not felt as such by the
man then, but still whatever is contained *in* an act,

the Divine Goodness can evolve *out of* it, and therefore in the world of the Spirit, when the act has
long ceased, or rather where it never was, the Divinity
and true dignity of the *motive,* of the will, is all that
is felt and seen, and then the exaltation and enjoyment are transcendent and ineffable."

SWEDENBORG'S WRITINGS [1]

" On Saturday I dined with Mr Coxe, at his office
in the City, and saw there the manuscript of the
'Apocalypsis Explicata,' three quarto volumes in
the Author's own writing. You may guess how
small and compact the writing is by the fact that
his three volumes of manuscript print into four
volumes ! The writing is very beautiful and extremely legible. I took the trouble after dinner
to make a facsimile of a short paragraph with the
style and tracing paper, so that I have got it very
exact indeed."

[2] " I am very glad you did not commence reading
the ' Apocalypse Revealed ' ; for, although it is
truly a wonderful book, I do feel that it is the most
severe and dry piece of reading I ever took up.
I have nearly finished the first volume, which I
consider conclusive of the fact that there is an
internal sense in the Scriptures of which the writer

[1] Letter to Miss Marsh, August 27, 1839.
[2] Letter to Miss Marsh, undated.

was cognizant, but still I only finish the book as a question of evidence. . . . I conceive that Swedenborg's book on ' The Last Judgment ' ought to be read before it, in order to make people in some way acquainted with the subject treated of. I should tell you that I am reading it out of a musty old translation printed in Manchester. The very sight of the book is repulsive, so I approach it under all sorts of disadvantages. I think that a new edition on good paper would have much assisted me, and ministered a delight to the senses, which is not to be despised as an assistance to the soul."

SWEDENBORG AND MATRIMONY [1]

" On Sunday I dined at Mr Tulk's and spent a very pleasant day. Mr Tulk read me a portion of a work he is writing on the Lord's Prayer. He also told me a very curious anecdote of Swedenborg. On what authority it rests, I know not, but as it was told me I tell it. Someone asked Swedenborg why he had never married. He replied either ' that he was married ' or that ' he had seen his future wife in the spiritual world.' He also named her and said she was a Countess Gildenberg." [2]

[1] Letter to Miss Marsh, September 24, 1839.

[2] Swedenborg's first love and its disappointment are related in Wilkinson's " Emanuel Swedenborg" (pp. 14-15 and 250, 251): " With regard to his first and only love, Emerentia Polhen, Swedenborg in his old age, as Tybeck relates, assured the daughters and sons-in-law of the former object of his affection, as they visited

Swedenborg's Manuscript [1]

" I am now writing an Introduction to the ' Hieroglyphic Key,' in which, in very brief, I shall attempt
to touch upon the Science of Correspondences in its
serial aspect: as a manifold, and not a simple or
(what is the same thing), an occult science. For a
manifold science involves the idea of love, reconcilia-
tion of parts, charity; whereas a *simplistic* science
is haughty, high and reserved."

Swedenborg's Chemistry [2]

" 'The Principles of Chemistry' is a rare book, and
only to be had either by advertising for it as wanted,
say in *Morning Light,* or by giving Mr Speirs a
commission to get it.

" May I briefly remark that you cannot, by
following modern science, enter Swedenborg's track.
This is nowhere more shewn than in Chemistry.
The *end* and *use* of modern chemistry is analytic
knowledge of substances, whether for manufacturing
purposes, or for exploration of nature. The quest
is for primitive substances; and when these are

---

him in his garden, that he could converse with their departed
mother whenever he pleased." It was told us by the late Mr Charles
Augustus Tulk, but we have no document for it, that our author
used to say that he had seen his allotted wife in the spiritual world,
who was waiting for him, and under her mortal name had been a
Countess Gyllenborg (*sic*)."

[1] Letter to Mr Henry James, September 18, 1847.
[2] Letter to Mr John Marten, March 19, 1896.

found, their combination or synthesis comes. The laws of this are greatly investigated.

" Swedenborg's was another Chemistry, of inviolate forms, with properties from the forms; as man and woman have properties from their forms : and there are no simple substances. Simple substances are the ultimates of destruction : atoms you can't cut. Swedenborg's Forms are simple or compound functions, which must be maintained in the Theory, because they are mineral-organic. The bed of all this is Geometry actuated, in each case, by a *central particular fire.*

" Beware of dismissing Light from your view of nature. Energy won't supply its place. Light and Heat are the unchangeable representants and correspondences of Love and Wisdom, divine."

EMERSON'S " SWEDENBORG OR THE MYSTIC "[1]

" I am much your debtor for a copy of your Poems transmitted to me by your London Publisher, and from which I have derived health and pleasure. I know of no writer equal to you for transporting the denizen of the city spiritually into the country, and giving him the benefit of ' that liberty, the air,' together with a thousand other needed enfranchisements. But I dare not attempt to criticize you. One thing, however, strikes me profoundly,

[1] Letter to Mr R. W. Emerson, March 1, 1841.

and I do not see any of your critics notice it : I mean your profound poetical analysis of natural and scientific truth. For instance, how sharply yet largely true your recount of the physiology of the loving *eye* in that Poem entitled ' Initial Love.' [1]

" But I must not trust myself to say more for fear I should awkwardly be paying you some intended compliment from which you might shrink with dislike.

" Although you state that your Swedenborgian shelves are full, I have ventured still to send through Mr Clapp a thin volume of the same series, hoping that you will gently squeeze it into a place among the rest. . . .

" Is your lecture on Swedenborg published yet ? If not, and if it is to appear as Copyright in England, might I suggest that, were it to be issued *per se*, it would probably command a very extensive sale among the readers of that Author in this country.

---

[1] " Leave his weeds and heed his eyes,—
All the rest he can disguise.
In the pit of his eyes a spark
Would bring back day if it were dark ;
And, if I tell you all my thought,
Though I comprehend it not,
In those unfathomable orbs,
Every function he absorbs.
He doth eat, and drink, and fish, and shoot,
And write, and reason, and compute,
And ride, and run, and have, and hold,
And whine, and flatter, and regret,
And kiss and couple and beget,
By those roving eyeballs bold."

I should be happy to do all I could to commend it to a large audience."

SWEDENBORG'S "HEAVEN AND HELL" TRANSLATED INTO ICELANDIC [1]

"DEAR DR WILKINSON,—I beg to acknowledge the receipt of your letter enclosing two others from your Icelandic friend. I will take the first opportunity of forwarding them to the Repository and obtain their insertion in the next number, if it be not at present too late; or if it be, they can appear in the number for November.

"I have no doubt the Committee of the Swedenborg Society will be rejoiced to receive the glad tidings they contain, and, for myself, I cannot but feel most humbly thankful to Divine Providence for such a result.

"I do not know when the Committee next meet, but if you have any proposition to make with respeet to the translation into Icelandic of the 'Heaven and Hell,' I have no doubt of its favourable reception by the Committee and the necessary funds being provided.

"If your mind is made up on this subject, I would suggest your writing a letter to me, as you did before, giving some idea of the amount of the funds and the time required, and engaging, as you

[1] Letter from the Rev. Augustus Clissold, September 11, 1871.

were kind enough to do before, that the translation
into Icelandic shall be a faithful one. This letter
I will then lay before the Committee, and I feel
sure they will be ready to carry out your wishes
and those of the Icelanders.—I am, dear sir, yours
very truly,   " AUGUSTUS CLISSOLD."

The translation was duly preformed by Mr Ion
a Hjaltalin.

CATHOLICITY [1]

" This morning's paper contains Cardinal Newman's
Address, on his reception of the Purple. It is
Liberalism in Religion. A great deal that he says
is too true ; but the error of Sect cannot be cured
by adopting Rome, which is the Sect of Sects ; and
her apostacy the cause of the divisions in Christendom
and of the great gulf in it, on the other side of which
stands the bold Realm of Infidelity. Unitary Truth
from Love, which can only come by a new Dispensation from the Lord, is the only Oneness that is needed
—or possible."

DR LIVINGSTONE [2]

" Dr Livingstone entered the spiritual world on
the 15th of last August. What a strange fire of
adventure possessed him, to spend all his old days in

[1] Letter to Mrs Wilkinson, May 13, 1879.
[2] Letter to Mrs Wilkinson, January 28, 1874.

battling with swamp and wood and wilderness after Geographical Truth ! It seems an *outré* genius ; and yet, if he was commissioned from within as the pioneer of African progress, so great an end elevates his direful wanderings into a religious life. Peace be with him now ! "

INFLUX [1]

" I have just finished 'Barnaby Rudge,' and a wonderful book it is. How the new Light and Love shine in it, and how the new Spiritual Power stoops down in it, and almost makes itself manifest for what it is ! Influx—influx is given to men as it was not given before."

NIAGARA [2]

" Let me say in these hurried words that Niagara, mighty and perpetual, suggests to me even more (in this mood of mine) than it shows to me. It even partly lulls and partly stuns me into sleep about its enormous self. And I think of what the Descent of things is ; of the Architecture that descends ; of the Holy City, New Jerusalem ; and in the immense rainbows that span the heaven over the Falls here ; that lie mile-wide on the river : that shimmer as they are fed by perpetual spray and mist, I remember,

[1] Letter to Mrs Wilkinson, August 24, 1872.
[2] Letter to Mrs Wilkinson, September 6, 1869.

" Her light was like unto a stone most precious " :
and in the Rainbows dissolved in the air I remember
the same : and in all, not omitting the vivid and
ever-varied thunders, and the huge sperm and
beauty of ever new Form, I catch a suggestion
of that substantial River of Influx which in
one little world and small Voice is the Holy
Ghost.

These are the thoughts I had of Descent ; very
different from those of Mont Blanc, or those of
Ascent."

DARWIN'S FUNCTIONS [1]

" I have just finished ' The Life and Letters of
Charles Darwin,' by his son. Mistaken, as I believe
he was, in discarding Revelation, and rejecting Deity
because he could not find Him out to perfection,
the life of the man leads me to think that there was
a providential purpose worked out by his permitted
wilfulness. One end seems to be that he brought the
whole mind of Europe down to consider facts, and
on them to crucify Dogmas. Had he understood the
' Doctrine of Uses,' as coming from above, he would
have begun a great fabric : but he would not have
done what he has done, and the opposing *Ecclesiasms*
would have resisted, which they are not now doing.
He has contributed to their death.

[1] Letter to Mr John Thomson, September 25, 1895.

Q

FICTION [1]

" What you say of Novels and their retreat into unlooked for Uses I heartily endorse. Without profanity, by fictional stories, everything in the sensual mind can be freely talked over, and anger from dogmas disappears where freedom reigns all round. The word 'Agnostic' is for this reason better than 'Atheist,' because its venom is withdrawn in its novelty of possibly pleaded harmlessness.

" Have you, in the *New Church Magazine* for July, seen my review of Richard Whiteing's ' Number 5 John Street ' ? He writes me that of the seventy great reviews he has had in the press of Great Britain and America my interpretation has given him more thought than all the rest, and that he keeps it by him to study it. . . . [2]

" I am rather tired now, after my four months' prayer, to be helped in my " Isis and Osiris in the Book of Respirations." For fifty years I have been on this theme in its general application of Breathing. Now I have been enabled to converse with it in most special embraces."

[1] Letter to the Rev. P. Melville, B.D., September 25, 1899.

[2] On March 28 of the same year, Wilkinson wrote to Dr Melville: " I am not going on with my little Essay on the Egypt of Correspondence. It has been interrupted by a very remarkable Book by Richard Whiteing, 'Number 5 John Street.' I have written a Swedenborgian View of it. It deserves it, for it is an inspiration, or refluxion for purposes of use, of the Hades within and above us. It may be published, and if so you shall see it. Mr Whiteing is an intimate friend of our house, and he may have been infected with the ' Apocalypse Revealed' which I have lent him."

CHAPTER III

WE have seen something of Garth Wilkinson's adoption of the practice of Homœopathy in the chapter devoted to his life. It occupied so large a place in his total of work done that, in a full consideration of the man, it needs to be treated in more detail.

The credit of founding a new method of drug-selection in the treatment of disease belongs to Samuel Hahnemann, who was born in 1755 and lived until 1843. Possessed of at least a double dose of " divine discontent " with the empiric practice of his day, Hahnemann recognized the dual action of drugs in the contradictory and confusing account of the effects of Cinchona, as given in a work on Materia Medica which he was engaged in translating from English into German. He investigated and developed the idea thus presented to him until he established his famous law *Similia similibus curentur*. The system of medicine based upon this law involves the proving of drugs upon healthy persons (Hahnemann's " Pure Materia Medica ") and the use of drug-symptoms thus developed as an index

244 JAMES JOHN GARTH WILKINSON

to the cure of similar disease-symptoms observed in the sick. As a logical correlative to the system upon which the drug was chosen, its dose for the sick is less than that sufficient to produce its characteristic effects in the healthy prover.

Partly by reason of the innate conservatism of the medical mind, partly through the bitter controversial methods of its discoverer, Homœopathy has laboured under professional discouragement from its first beginning to the present day. It may claim to have profoundly modified practice : the bleeding lancet is no longer to be found in the waistcoat pocket of every medical student; the significance of the barber's pole and basin has become a matter of archæology; the old lengthy and murderous prescription is almost extinct; drugs and doses introduced by Hahnemann and his followers are in daily use. But the system is far from general recognition; and those who systematically follow its law are still made to remember that, though they are in the medical profession and enjoy such scanty privileges as that profession bestows, they are far from sharing its blood-brotherhood.

The introduction of Homœopathy evoked a storm of protest. The profit of those who made shrines in precious metals to the old gods was endangered, and those who taught the new way were threatened with the magistrate. Dr Quin, who brought the Hahnemannian doctrine and practice to England in

1837, found patients in plenty at once and professional followers more slowly. These latter had to face opposition both overt and covert, professional ostracism and outrageous criticism. They were knaves or fools, lucky if they escaped condemnation under both headings. If a patient died under the care of one of their number, it was darkly hinted that a verdict of manslaughter should follow. It needed, therefore, no slight resolution, no tepid conviction, in the man who professed himself a homœopath in the early " forties." The unpopularity of a cause had, however, never deterred Wilkinson from espousing it for reason shown : and at the time of his conversion he had been long dissatisfied alike with the ordinary practice of his profession and his own position therein. Pitchforked into the study of medicine by his father when a mere boy, sickened at the crude practice to which he was introduced in his apprenticeship, he engaged in the struggle for maintenance without any of that timely assistance which ensures a good beginning and goes far to further, if it cannot command, a prosperous career. It is little wonder that the early days of Wilkinson's practice were not marked either by enthusiasm on his part or any greedy acceptance on the part of the patient public. The work of a general practitioner in the " thirties " approximated much more to that of the chemist than is to-day the case : he had to recommend the copious consumption of physic, for it was from physic that he derived profit. Wilkinson was possessed of two qualities incompatible to the foundation of a successful practice upon such lines, a conscience and " a horror of promiscuous drugging." His enthusiasm was reserved for work in matters Swedenborgian, and he eked out what came to him through labour in that capacity by means of professional work repugnant alike to his taste and his higher nature. There is no statement in his correspondence which gives a date when homœopathy first came under Wilkinson's notice, but a letter from a friend in 1844 congratulates him on his intention to investigate the subject. In December of the same year Wilkinson writes to Mr Henry James that his only son is dangerously ill with bronchitis and whooping cough. " We have committed him to Homœopathy, and called in Dr Durnford who has been very kind in his attentions, although but little marked improvement has yet taken place." Two years later, he is found writing to his absent wife of a discussion with a medical friend who " appeared in no way bigoted against the subject." But he gives a lively and presumably accurate account of the means by which he was brought to consider Hahnemann's system of treatmemt, in " War, Cholera and the Ministry of Health," written in 1854. The pamphlet which perhaps gives the best example of Wilkinson's " early manner," virtually aimed at recommending Homœopathy to recognition by the Public Services.[1]

" The fact is that nurses have a great many things put upon them which either ought to be undone, or the doctors ought to do them for themselves. Many a medicine given to children is so chokingly horrible that a medical practitioner ought to be present to count the pulse and to watch the countenance ; just as is properly the case at a military flogging. In my old days I have seen a nurse resign the trembling spoon or cup to the doctor, and say in the boldness of humane terror : ' Sir, give it yourself.' My own conversion to homœopathy was attended with one of these experiences. Our eldest child, a baby then, was attacked in the night with a sudden bronchitis, attended with great wheezing and oppression. My wife and I sat on end in bed in sanitary conjugal quorum. I *ordered* ipecacuanha wine as an emetic, and I went downstairs to the surgery and fetched it. There it stood by the bedside, and the question was, who should give it ? My wife said nothing, and I broke a short silence by observing that the medicine was there. She then said : ' Well ! ' and another silence ensued. I too said ' Well ! ' and again we were silent. At length Mrs W. said : ' What are you going to do ? ' I said : ' What are *you* going to do ? " she said she was not going to give the child that medicine. I felt indignant in all my

[1] " War, Cholera and the Ministry of Health," p. 27, 1854.

professional frame, and I told her that the ordering of medicine was the doctor's department, that it was the business of mothers and nurses to give it. She replied that I was not only doctor here, but also father and nurse, and that I must do it or it would not be done; and she added also, that she had no faith in that stuff; and furthermore that she was glad now that I had seen at home what burdens were daily laid on parents and nurses when I went away from house to house, leaving such things to be transacted between my visits. I thought of the denunciation in the Gospel against those who lay on grievous burdens, which themselves will not touch with one of their fingers; and I could not but admire her disobedience. But she did not stop here, but told me that for long (she had hinted this before) she had felt a repugnance to my practice, and that this very occasion was sent, partly to oblige me to look into that new thing called Homœopathy. The upshot of the particular case was that my wife gave a piece of ipecacuanha, such as would pass through the eye of a needle, to the child; and a good and homœopathic remedy it was; after which, the oppression of the breathing passed away. The circumstance made an impression on my mind, and I now record it, being sure as day that, humble and simple as it is, it will leave a mark on the minds of mothers. Think, then, mothers, fathers and nurses, what a blessing it is to you to get rid at one blow of all these difficult and painful duties which the old practice enjoins upon you ! "

In December 1850 he writes to his father of gradually introducing homœopathy into his practice, and says that " nearly all the little success I have enjoyed has arisen from and in the new practice." In 1852 he writes more strongly on the subject.

" My business increases beyond expectation : it seems going on rapidly for £2000 a year. Homœopathy, into which Emma compelled me, has for the first time caused me really to love my noble Profession. To me now there is no calling like it. It brings down not only riches, but, what is far more, blessings upon him that exercises it aright ; and as for intellectual advancement, which I have always loved, I have learned to be sure that a man's own business is the finest school in which his mind can be trained. The truths of Medicine are, then, those which above all others I pray God to show me— in order that I may find healing on their wings.

" Of course, with so large a practice, I require to undergo many expenses. . . . But practice increases far more rapidly than expense, and I am in great hopes of being able, after this year, to put by something handsome for a rainy day.

" You will not be surprised to hear that I have no leisure for any avocations but those of my profession. It engages me morning, noon and night ; excepting on Sundays, when I never *go out*, if I can avoid it.

However, in the course of my rides, I make many cursory but agreeable studies, particularly in Botany, respecting which I cherish some designs. Homœopathy has led me to the study of the old Herbals of various countries, and I see in them an unlimited extension of the Homœopathic medicine. England is particularly rich in this kind of lore, and it is only to be lamented that in our accredited books of Botany, this really useful department of knowledge of the vegetable world is either left out or treated with contempt. But all things will come in time. At present I am studying the Mistletoe, with a view to its medical use."

In the same year he wrote to Mr James : [1]

" My life now is for the most part a routine. Practice increases month by month ; and the prospects of income are good. The pleasures of skill also attend me, whenever God gives any of the skill. What is best, I take a leading interest in my dear Medicine, and especially in Homœopathy : and I reckon myself truly fortunate to be able at length to connect my mind to my daily work ; and to see in the latter a most ample field for the exercise of my thoughts. I am even not without hopes that I may be able to improve practice somewhat.

" If it please God to afford me the possibility, I shall take one summer holiday in New York, if only to shake you and yours by the hand. It is a part of

[1] Letter to Mr Henry James, November 14, 1852.

my medical creed that a medical man cannot do justice to his year unless he recreates himself for a few weeks in the best season. This I shall act upon as soon as I can. And your country shall have *one* of my first fortnights.[1]

"My chief studies at present are Homœopathy, Botany, as connected with the popular medical use of Plants, the Herbals of all nations and their availability for practice; lastly, the physical and physiological and the pathogenetic characters of substances, and the correspondence between these various characters. Thus, for example, I want to see in the growth and character of a plant the very double of the effects which it produces upon the animal body. Now this, with practice and Northern Languages, is what my little life is about."

It is a scheme of pursuits large enough to occupy the mind of a busy man. Wilkinson had "found himself" medically, just as he had "found himself" theologically some years earlier; and it is plain that the theology and the medicine have an essential connection. It is plain, too, that the stricter limits of homœopathy, which demand that the drugs prescribed shall have been proved on the healthy body, were not entirely to his taste. In this, as in all things, Wilkinson was eclectic and transcendental, ready to advance beyond the letter of his master when he had himself assimilated the spirit.

[1] It was not until 1869, however, that Wilkinson visited the United States.

[1] " Do you know that I am going out of the bounds of Homœopathy in the use of medicaments ? I find that the old Herbals give note of a number of plants and the like, useful for certain maladies ; and the use descended from ancient time and well attested. Now, what but pedantry should prevent anyone from curing by this prestige ? Why not prepare the herbs Homœopathically, and use them by tradition ? When they have been also proved upon the healthy body, so much the better ; but why wait for that ? The fact of cure is just as scientific as, and more direct than, the fact of pathogenesy. Here is a matter that has been neglected, and that I must work, as being of import to human health."

In the meantime, if Wilkinson proclaimed himself unconcerned with strict orthodoxy towards the creed of his adoption, he was made conscious of his unorthodoxy towards the traditional practice of his profession ; and that too was a matter which troubled him little.

[2] " The medical profession is indeed bitter against Homœopathy : and they are to be excused, for they are considerable losers by it. The Homœopathic practitioners, on the other hand, are in a state of equanimity and good humour, and find it not very difficult to love their enemies, when the public and success are so markedly in their own favour. Here

[1] Letter to Mr Henry James, December 30, 1852.
[2] Letter to his Father, January 28, 1852.

in this neighbourhood I have no competitors : the old practitioners do me no harm, but compete seriously with each other : and I, by sitting still, reap the benefit of their divisions. This is going on at an increased ratio every year, and must, in the end, work a vital alteration in the position of what now regards itself as Orthodox Medicine. *Apropos*, however, of which orthodoxy, it is as new in point of time, if not of truth, as Homœopathy itself. For, were the Garths and the Boerhaves to peep down upon us now, they would never recognize the present Rulers of Medicine as their lineal descendants."

His reply to his experience of the "Odium Medicum" was the delivery and publication of an Address on "Unlicensed Medicine," a whole-hearted attack on his own profession, wherein he charged it with narrowness of mind and self-interested policy, with neglect of progress and with surgical mutilation undertaken for the profit of the operator rather than that of the patient. He advocated reform by complete discharterment of medicine, leaving it free for all men to practise at their peril, subject to punishment for recklessness or culpable negligence. It was written, we may surmise, rather for the sake of the indictment than in any expectation of securing either conviction or reform. Concerning it, he wrote : [1]

" I will send you the Address on 'Unlicensed

[1] Letter to his Father, December 15, 1855.

Medicine' when I get a copy : I have none by me, but have ordered a supply from the Publishers. In estimating the *prudence* of the Tract, it is to be borne in mind that I am not in a usual position ; but that the other school of Medicine already bans me and all similar persons. Did I belong to the established class, such an address would indeed be the height of imprudence."

Upon the question of dose in treatment, Wilkinson was among what even the homœopaths reckon " high dilutionists," prescribing almost always on a centesimal scale and usually far along it. In a " lay " consideration of his medical work, it will be enough to quote his opinion as given to a " lay " correspondent, and to add that his habitual use of drugs tended ever to become more and more immaterial.

[1] " To what you say about small doses Homœopathic and large doses ditto, I have only one thing to answer, that I find my minute potions do their work—surely, swiftly, and sweetly. If others find bigger things do the same, there is not any quarrel between us. But I do aver and maintain my own position. Every day's practice confirms me in the thought that, if the right remedy is hit, the quantity is a secondary affair ; though also the quantity, in that case, by all the rules of causes, may be smaller than in the other case—of inexacter skill.

[1] Letter to Mr Henry James, February 8, 1855.

"But my object, my grand wish, in the little Book,[1] is to show that Medicine can be organized and applied to nations by Homœopathy, and as yet by no other claimant. This argument, if it be impregnable, casts back a powerful confirmation on Homœopathy itself, and thrills it through with public virtue.

"*You*, more than any other man, led me into Homœopathy, and if you are lapsing away from it, I shall think it my duty to take your Senility into custody and to keep you by me in an old man's chair of credulity, until you can start young again into faith."

But the main point of interest in Wilkinson's adoption of Homœopathy lies in the similarity which can be plainly seen in his theological and medical creed. The doctrine of correspondences is the working key of the New Church attitude toward God and conduct. In matters medical, the correspondence of drug effects and disease effects is the whole of the Homœopathic practice. This similarity was a striking one to Wilkinson, whose attachment to medicine had never been strongly marked. The convinced and enthusiastic followers of Swedenborg found the system of Hahnemann a scientific statement of the doctrine of correspondences in terms of medicine. He did not, however, adopt it *per saltum* on purely theoretic grounds, but examined

[1] "War, Cholera and the Ministry of Health."

it and tested it on his patients. By degrees he found himself leaning ever more toward the homœopathic law, and ever less addicted to the routine practice of the time : patients flocked to him : he was for the first time happy in being " able to connect his mind to his work."   Yet in this, as in other things, he stood alone. There were, he felt, possibilities of extension and development in Homœopathy ; and he was characteristically eager to make the summit of Hahnemann's attainment the " jumping off place " into a new conquest over disease by a transcendental extension of the law of similars. But it was the doctrine of correspondences which made and kept him a Homœopathist ; and traces of the bond between his religious and medical creed are constantly cropping up in the letters and books which he wrote. It is much in evidence in the following quotation from " Swedenborg among the Doctors " an open letter to Dr Cooper at whose house Wilkinson had been invited to a medical *symposium* in 1895. He was unable to attend, but sent what he afterwards expanded into a tract to represent his views.

" To command the country of the soul, that is, the human body, a military intellect, seeing the anarchy and disorder of scientism, its want of a Ruling Soul, could not but discern as a strategic necessity, that it was necessary to lay down new *ways* by which he might be led to such unrecognized Ruler, and gain access to her palace, and support

and sanction from her power. Every march of
humanity requires new roads if there are none laid
down already. Hahnemann, coming into empirical
and chaotic medicine, found an old disused road
in Hippocrates, ' *Similia similibus curentur*,' and
following it resolutely, he founded a new medical
Kingdom. Our Art, Homœopathy, is thus, by
virtue of having a mental highway through it, a
stable possession of the rational faculty. Let this
instance, familiar to us, show the importance, or
rather indispensable necessity, of doctrinal Road-
making; we may say, of iron roads.

" Under stress of this, Swedenborg gratified what
was then his life's love, the prosecution of the quest
of the soul by rational divination of her attributes
from her faculties in the body. The new ways by
which he must travel are not, however, easy to him
to find. He has ' to discover, disengage and bring
them forth, by the most intense application and
study.' They are new doctrines, for doctrines always
lead, guide and lead on and on : true doctrines
namely. These might always be summed up in
the injunction, ' *Similia, similibus divinentur* ' or
' *interpretentur*.' ' They are the doctrines of forms,
of order and degrees, of series and society, of communication and influx, of correspondence and representation, and of modification.' These doctrines
or teachings are the way to a Rational Psychology,
or approximate knowledge of the Soul."

R

The same view is expressed in a more practical connection in the following letter to an old friend : [1]

" DEAR FRIEND,—I rejoice to hear that you are walking miles, and that you have a rest from newspapers and books. But I cannot divine why you should not cure yourself by homœopathic coincidences which are natural and scientific correspondences, and which follow the divine way of ceasing medicinally first to do any evil, and then are gifted to do good. Were you to send to the homœopathic chemist in Glasgow for a half-ounce bottle of *Antim. Tart.* pilules, and take three, night and morning, in a wineglassful of hot water, you would, in my belief, cease to be the slave of damp, and brain would animate, and lung would respire. Who can say that the Lord's arm is interfered with by using the vanishing point of medicine, when it becomes mental scientific correspondences ? Hot bricks, etc., etc., are means ; but so also is that practice which takes up deadly serpents, and forbids their harming and then does their good. For they have good. As E. S. says, they absorb malignities.—Yours,

" J. J. GARTH WILKINSON."

Correspondences and homœopathy are again correlated in this letter to a friend whose daughter was in trouble with curvature of the spine. It is interest-

[1] Letter to Mr J. Thomson, June 7, 1898.

ing, too, to see that the writer, at the age of 84, is ready to endorse the bicycle for the use of women.

" I sympathize with you heartily in your perplexity about your dear Daughter's treatment. You know I am a resolved Homœopath, and so far as drugs go, I am confirmed in this name by the immeasurably greater harmlessness and success of the treatment by the science of correspondences intuitively and experimentally given through Hahnemann. So I should certainly advise medicine in that line in spinal curvature. Other treatment also. But without knowing the extent of the curvature, it is difficult to suggest or sanction. . . .

" With respect to Cycling, I am not at all disposed to endorse her opinion that no woman should cycle. It is founded on no experience; and against it there is the fact that women cycle better than men. Deprived of the masculine seat on the horse, why should not woman be bilateral on these terrene skates of steel ? My granddaughters, just returned from Coblenz, tell me that their brother, Captain Pertz, holds that the ladies beat the officers, their husbands, in cycling. But evidently in a young lady of 17 with a weak spine, fatigue should be avoided."

Wilkinson's spiritualized and transcendal view of medicine, and the essential unity of his theological and medical outlook come out very clearly too in the following letter.

[1] " I received your fine volume, ' The Twelve Tissue Remedies of Schussler,' soon after the arrival of your letter, and I have every reason to thank you for it. I have read Part I. with attention, and use the Body of the Book in my now small opportunities of practice. And later on, if my year of life be still prolonged, your Remarks may help me greatly in a few words which I desire to leave respecting Homœopathy.

" Schussler is vague both in his idea of the twelve salts in their existence in the blood, and also as regards the causation of the effects of the same salts as administered in his 6th triturations. Only one man that I know of propounded an organic view, which at last, with a vital end internal to it, must be the clear and central intuition. That one man was Swedenborg. His statement that the atom of common salt is the basement on which the blood-globule is built up—the dead, useful, natural world of it—assigns place and function to this cell-salt. And the further information that there are aerial and etherial salts corresponding and similarly basic in the higher blood-architectures is a higher stretch than any doctrine of dilutions. What may be the ultimate fate of this spiritually-ingenious theory? At least it must stimulate thoughts. Whatever the bone of the blood, can it be diseased, so as to set up a crooked blood-spine, involving a weak nerve

[1] Letter to Dr Boericke, October 19, 1893.

influx and dwarfish deformed nature in the atomic blood itself ? (One) such as a weak deformed spine may involve in the general body ?

"And then how does an infinitesimal cell-salt correct aberrations of such salts in the organism ? Here we want a theory of Homœopathy; for Schussler's salts all act by their likeness to their fellow-salts suffering and crying out in the body. Through my dear R. E. Dudgeon, I have just re-perused the 'Organon,' translated by him; but Hahnemann's explanation of Homœopathy is not a likely one, for how can the slight monition of an infinitesimal dose be a more powerful state than the diseased action which it fronts and routs ? David's pebble from the Brook which smote Goliath was not naturally stronger than he, but spiritually. So Homœopathy needs a spiritual, or natural-spiritual, explanation. So also does Catalysis. A doctrine of regeneration is needed. *That* can alter things from the smallest beginnings, and rectify a salt that has lost its character, and make the blood upright. To follow out this Swedenborgian opening will be the work of future time. I want to think of it, if my time allows.

"The salts in Plants must be prepared by and in organization for acting peculiarly on animal organization: and mineral salts themselves must have a peculiar field.

"On the subject of plant-salts, I will mention that

I have long used the silica which is deposited in the bottoms of the manifold cases of the large bamboos in India: and, having some, I will send you a specimen. I have used it with success where silica is indicated, but especially in acute, rather than in chronic, cases."

Wilkinson's scientific contributions to the literature of the school of medicine to which he belonged have been enumerated in the chapter which deals with his biography: they were marked by all his usual power of expression and definition of aim. He contributed also to the number of drugs used by the homœopath. On one of his Icelandic journeys he was struck by the frequency of caries and necrosis among the natives living in the volcanic regions and attributed the prevalence of these diseases to the use of water which had percolated through lava. Recognizing the bearing of the homœopathic law upon this observation, he was led to prepare and prescribe Hekla lava as a drug for similar cases otherwise induced; and the drug has justified its selection and maintained its place in its own limited field. In 1857 he also introduced to use Glanderine and Farcine, two nosodes or products from Veterinary diseases. The use of such things was at that time vilified and derided by those who opposed homœopathy, but Wilkinson lived to see the age of Koch's various tuberculins and of the antidiptheritic serum. The articles in which he advocated the use of these drugs may be found by the curious in " The British Journal of Homœopathy."

But, after all, the work of the practising physician can only be traced partially in the professional press. When once Wilkinson had embraced homœopathy, he recognized himself and was speedily recognized by others as highly gifted in the treatment of disease. From that time forward his practice was assured, and he numbered people of influence and position among his patients. Indeed, to the time of his death, there were those who would not allow him to retire altogether from attending them : there was always a residuum who refused to believe that he could not and would not help them in their bodily ailments. From 1850 to 1880 his practice was a large one : after the death of Mrs Wilkinson in 1886, he withdrew from it to a great extent. Reckoning from his qualification in 1834, he was actively engaged in medical work for fifty-two years : but to the end, as we have said, he was more or less in touch with the treatment of disease.

Perhaps, however, there was never a practitioner of medicine who was less a member of the profession at heart. Almost from the first he would have dischartered that profession and have thrown the treatment of the sick open to all who chose to engage in it, holding them equally responsible whether formally qualified or not. Degrees and diplomas would have conveyed no privilege, had Wilkinson been allowed his way. Surgery was ever an abomination to him. He not only abstained from practising it himself; but he would have surrounded its practice by others with narrow restrictions and have checked its development: its abuse, as he reckoned it, would have met with immediate and proportionate punishment. His quarrel with chartered and licensed medicine gradually crystallized itself around three subjects, vaccination, vivisection and the working of the Contagious Diseases Act. It is necessary that we should deal briefly with Wilkinson's action with regard to each of these subjects.

When his sister contracted smallpox in Wilkinson's bachelor establishment, in the early summer of 1839, he wrote to his fiancée: " On Friday morning I procured some lymph, and vaccinated all the inmates, including myself; and I am now most desirous that you should be placed in safety by the same process. How and when this is to be done we must endeavour to determine." So it is clear that at this time he was not opposed to either the theory or practice of Jenner's inoculation, which had then been before the world for some forty years.

His aversion can be told in his own words: " The early history of my opposition to Vaccination is, briefly, this—I had not considered Vaccination a question; but practised it when required. About 1865 the Countess de Noailles assailed my conscience on the subject, and her earnestness forced me to study it. She was backed by the late Mrs Gibbs, then Miss Griffiths. Through Miss Griffiths, I sent the following message to Madame de Noailles :—' Tell her Ladyship that the question is comparatively unimportant. Vaccination is an infinitesimal affair. Its reform will come in with greater reforms.' I also wrote to Madame that the only short way of getting rid of the medical vested interest was by paying half a million or a million of money down to the Profession, and buying the slaves, the people, out, as the West Indian Blacks were brought out.

" After-studies extending over eighteen years have convinced me that I was wrong in my estimate of the smallness of the Vaccination question compared with other Evils. As forced upon every British Cradle, I see it is a monster instead of as a Poisonous Midge ; a Devourer of Nations. As a Destroyer of the Honesty and Humanity of Medicine, which is through it a deeply degraded Profession. As a Tyrant which is the Parent of a brood of Tyrants, and through Pasteur and his like a Universal Pollution Master. As a Ghoul which sits upon Parliament, and enforces Contamination by Law, and prepares the way for endless violations of personal liberty and sound sense at the bidding of cruel experts. Not denying other forms of Social Wickedness, I now, after careful study, regard Vaccination as one of the greatest and deepest forms, abolishing the last hope and resort of races, the new-born soundness of the Human Body." [1]

The first trace of this fierce opposition discoverable in Wilkinson's private correspondence occurs in a letter to his wife, dated February 23, 1870.

" There is, I hear, no truth in what the Paper says about Government and the Vaccination Laws. A storm is brewing such as they little expect. The cases of dire injury from Vaccination are multiplying, and the cases of *violated parents*, who, rightly or wrongly it matters not, are agonized about their little ones. Yesterday, Mrs —— got Miss —— to ask me my opinion about Vaccination. They insist upon doing her children, not yet out of whooping cough, or fining her ! The thing is too inconceivably abominable to last. Let whoso will be protected (?) by Vaccination be Vaccinated : but is it in this day that others, against their hearts' blood and their often terrible experiences and their convictions, should be compelled ? Mrs —— was moved to ask me by hearing such sad results from Vaccination in her own circle. I advised her not to have her child vaccinated."

Wilkinson gives two cases in his essay on Compulsory Vaccination which may explain his attitude toward the practice. The first of these appears from the context to have occurred in 1863.

" Miss Edith Hutchinson, of Kensington, was

[1] W. White, " The Story of a Great Delusion," p. 549.

vaccinated by the late eminent Dr Joseph Laurie. The arm swelled enormously, and was hard like wood. After a month it subsided, and then a putrid thrush occurred, which disappeared after some weeks. The disease was next transferred to the abdomen and its lymphatic system; and she died of great purulent collections in its cellular tissues, the matter, putrescent, voided by the bowels. I attended the later stages of the case with Dr L. Vaccination, careful conscientious vaccination, did it, as plainly as fire burns. . . . Another case. My coachman's child was vaccinated, and took it with erysipelas, which overspread the body. The mother, who was nursing it, took the erysipelas, and both nearly died of it. I assert that this result of two long and all but fatal illnesses was, in a poor man's house, due to vaccination, and consequently due to Parliament."

Wilkinson gave evidence before the House of Commons' Committee on Vaccination in 1871. He showed how, endowed and lucrative, the futility of vaccination was concealed and denied, and how reliance on its supposed efficacy paralyzed improvement in treatment. He wrote pamphlet after pamphlet against the evil as he saw it. A brief specimen of his plain speaking, from his " Human Science, good and evil, and its Works " (1876) will suffice.

" This is blood assassination, and like a murderer's

life. The point, however, here is that this amazing
act is the homicidal insanity of a whole profession ;
and the reader is requested to study the correlation
of this sin with the horrible methods of acquiring
physiology now in vogue, and which surely prepare
the minds of men for similar darkness and its deeds
in medical practice."

But Wilkinson's zeal did not exhaust itself in his
public writings. It constrained him also in many
seemingly minor matters.

In 1874 he is found writing to a candidate for
the Coronership of his division of London as follows:—

" I am solicited to vote for you for Coroner. I
do not vote for Dr H. (1) because a medical
coroner is not desirable; and (2) because Dr H. is
so identified with vaccination prosecutions that his
impartiality in cases of death from vaccination
could not be expected. How do you stand upon this
question ?

" Mr John Bright declares the Compulsory Vaccination Law to be ' monstrous,' and that it ought
to be repealed. One way of demonstrating its
monstrosity to the world is by fairly recording
its malfeasances in the verdicts of Coroners' juries
impartially charged by Coroners. A public word
from you on this point is desirable."

He interrogated the parliamentary candidates
in the same spirit, nor did his influential acquaint-
ances escape.

[1] " DEAR MR BRIGHT,—In earnest petition I
address you on the Compulsory Vaccination question.
On that subject you have expressed opinion twice,
and your views have been circulated through the
press. You said the first time, ' The law is monstrous,
and ought to be repealed.' And you write to Mr
Tebb, ' I think your case one of great hardship, but
I fear I can do nothing to help you. These repeated
penalties are, in my view, most unjust, and I wish
the law were changed."

" I cannot understand that your feeling against
a ' monstrous ' law, with its ' most unjust ' penalties,
should produce your last expression of opinion.
You cannot help Mr Tebb personally, and he does
not expect it. But what we do expect is that when
John Bright finds a law monstrous and wishes its
repeal, and when his little finger, stoutly raised,
would encourage and help the whole of the persecuted
against that law, justice and mercy, as of old, as for
Ireland, as for India, should move him ; and silence,
be it ever so much desired by him, should be greatly
broken.

" It is not by ' fearing that you can do nothing
to help ' that you have been the friend of the poor
and oppressed since first I heard you as a young
man in the Anti-Corn-Law Agitation. It is not
in the ignominious night-cap of such fearing
that your great sword of words has slept when

[1] Letter to Mr John Bright, December 17, 1877.

public evil was to be hewed down in the House of Commons.

" Arise, and give us some of the fire of your true heart here, in the name of the Lord, and He will keep your heart young, and chase all fears in other needful contests for the people.—Your friend,

"J. J. GARTH WILKINSON."

It is not clear what pronouncement by Mr Ruskin gave origin to this vigorous rejoinder from Wilkinson.

[1] " I have no right to rejoin to so masterful a dismissal as you give to the subject of vaccination. But pardon me for remarking that I care nothing for ' Codes of Lymph,' but abjure them ; and am only concerned to protect the prime stream of all, the blood of children, from pollution ; and the prime air of all, the liberty of affection and conscience in the home, from suffocation.

" Your Art Temple will stand on legs and not on fantasies when you are not ashamed to take as alternate pillars the substantial foundations of human good. And you will rebuke the Circe of Art, instead of aiding and abetting her, and will teach artists to be men, when you traverse their Art with religious duties involving their care and attention to many unpleasant every-day disciplines, which are the only correctives of Art against worldliness, luxury and selfishness."

[1] Letter to Mr John Ruskin, July 1, 1878.

Wilkinson made many lasting friendships among the enthusiastic opponents of Compulsory Vaccination. Among these were Professor Siljeström, writer of several Swedish tracts upon this subject, who died in 1892, and Mr William Young, whose work, as editor of the *Vaccination Tracts*, Wilkinson took up after his death and concerning whom Wilkinson wrote the following biographical notice for an Anti-Vaccination journal :—

"THE LATE MR WILLIAM YOUNG.

"Excepting that new men are often sent when public exigency calls for them, it is difficult to imagine how the gap caused by the decease of William Young can be filled from the ranks of the opponents of vaccination. He has stood in the front, and if not the foremost of all, it was rather because of his social station than from any defect of quality as a leader.

"He was a chemist and druggist, and kept a shop. What did this imply when he joined the movement against vaccination ? I knew him well with a large and increasing family. It was a tolerably flourishing shop in the Harrow-road. It fell down from plain causes. The medical men in the neighbourhood refused to send their prescriptions to the counter of an anti-vaccinationist. They 'boycotted' his shop. He was driven from it ; and was drifted along from neighbourhood to neighbourhood partly by the same cause. His poverty compelled each act of movement. But he was a real nobleman in every shop, true as steel to his convictions. He lived the truths he knew, and made them good. He belonged to the new comity—to the new order.

"I was associated with him in the *Vaccination Tracts*. In the preparation of these he always furnished me with a draft plan of each tract, and suggested several of the pieces. But for him the series would not have been completed. His urgency moved it on and fed it with useful suggestions of matter. His gentleness and modesty eliminated differences of design, and produced equal authority between us. Though suffering from something like want all the time, he did the work with no expectation of even common wage.

"With a very frail body, he did not ask himself how he was, but what the day's work was? So his industry was out of all proportion to his bodily strength, as the most of us equate the industry and the strength. He did not do more than he was able, because he knew the law that the ability is given in the doing. Every fresh occasion, and they were incessantly arising, called forth a wise and cogent word from him. Could the series of his articles and leaflets be collected, they would form a volume still useful to the cause, and displaying a heart full of sympathy with outraged fathers, mothers, and infants, and a head with a statesman-like vision of what would come to medical authority, and to Governments that aided and abetted it.

" Nor was his attention or insight confined to the vaccination tyranny, but he saw the downward career of State-established medicine, and noted the steps of the ladder which it is preparing for itself into the abyss. He divined its alliance with Pasteur ; and it is only a few weeks since I had a communication from him to make me acquainted with the New Youth recorded by Brown-Sequard for himself from the seed of dogs.

" He died, upon the whole, a neglected man ; but not more neglected than in most cases where rare unselfishness, humility, and honesty are combined with poverty, in pleading, irrespective of all personal consequences, the destruction of aggressive tyranny, and the furthering of public good, especially for the voiceless and the wailing, for the poor and the needy. The monument of their emancipation and bettering will rise for him, nay, has risen for him, but not in these climates, and not in their cathedrals.

" He has entered into his rest,' as they say. A man, however, of no hurry, making no over-estimate of what single human efforts can do in any age of visible self-will and its down-rush, he can help us from a higher ground to patience and perseverance through the yet long night, and to a new youth

s

of trust to God in ourselves, and to God and ourselves, rather than to the confirmed senility of Royal Commissions. Herein, we divine, will be a part of his Rest.

"'No flowers' may well be underscored in such an obituary. His path was not a flowery one; certainly not 'the primrose path to the everlasting bonfire.' He trod on thorns to make the way smooth and innocent for other people. If he can whisper now he might say, 'Not flowers, but everywhere Fruits.' And I will say what he never said, 'Ye who can, be personally fruitful here; ye who have been with him in this holy cause of anti-vaccination, think of the home left desolate now; think of his wife and children, in poverty now because of his life-long devotion to the interests of all homes and parental rights; and of love and conscience consecrate come part of your abundance, or your 'two mites,' to succour with money-offerings—yes, with money—those he loved, and who sorely need your assistance."

"Honour be to the noble memory of William Young!"

Many will consider that the agitation against the Compulsory Vaccination of Infants was misguided and futile : but few will deny to those who took the leading part in it that they were thoroughly honest in their convictions and earnest in their efforts, or that the ultimate outcome of their work in the recognition of the " conscientious objector " transcended anything which might, in the early days, have been expected from it. Right or wrong in his contentions, Wilkinson's attitude was forthright, insistent and uncompromising throughout; and to his work may be credited no small share of the result attained.

Remarks of somewhat the same character may be made concerning the share which Wilkinson took in opposing the practice and legal licence of experiments on living animals. His condemnation of vivisection was heart-felt and outspoken, as was his way, but we know of no instance where he perverted truth or imparted prejudice. He wrote some fugitive tracts on the subject, but his most reasoned pronouncement will be found running through " On Human Science, Good and Evil, and its Works; and on Divine Revelation and its Works and Sciences," which appeared in 1876, the year in which the " Vivisection Act " became law. Wilkinson held strong views as to the limitations of science; his tendency was to mistrust chemical and physical bases for vital processes; and this for him discounted the value of the results of vivisection. But had he held the general opinion of his profession as to the value of those results, he would still have regarded the processes by which they were attained as impious and profane in the deepest sense. It is not necessary to quote at length from his published writings upon the subject: it will suffice to give evidence of his feeling concerning it from his private correspondence.

When Professor Tafel was bringing out his monumental edition of Swedenborg's work upon " The Brain," he received from Wilkinson hearty and ungrudging assistance which was, by Wilkinson's own wish, only acknowledged generally, without mention of its extent or scope. The following extracts from letters show Wilkinson's anxiety that Swedenborg's name should not be brought to bear in support of vivisection :—

[1] " I have just received the enclosed, which I think you ought to read. I foresee that, without care be exercised, Swedenborg's citation of horribly cruel experiments on living animals will prejudice his name in a way that nothing else has done, with all those who uphold humanity to animals in this country; which is the stronghold of the ever-increasing feeling against the atrocities of scientism. My belief is that Swedenborg gained nothing for his intuitions or inductions from the atrocious vivisections which he cites. He flung them down as a basis, but did not want them, except that they were so much ' experience.' The whole love of his writings is against the scientism of mere curiosity as regards living beings ; and his theology continually

[1] Letter to Dr Tafel, April 11, 1882.

denounces the scientism of the *Proprium* as the greatest mental antagonist to true perception."

[1] "I have no intention of writing a Preface to your work. All I should wish to do, with your approval, is to give, in one paragraph, which you may describe as a private communication from me, my view of Swedenborg's possible standpoint with regard to vivisection. To state that what he has introduced into his work on the Brain does not show what his position would be in the Vivisection controversy of the present day. I do not think you would object to this. Also, in the same pages, you might confute it if you saw fit."

[2] "I want you to read carefully the enclosed pamphlet by Lawson Tait, which is the strongest professional attack that has yet been made on Vivisection. You once spoke to me of the ' abuse of Vivisection ': this pamphlet goes all the way to show that there is no such thing in a good sense as the Use of Vivisection. . . . It is a most serious subject, and one may well hesitate before letting the inference go forth that Swedenborg would now, when the subject has been opened up, be reckoned among the Vivisectors."

[3] "I thank you very much for your letter on Vivisection as related to Swedenborg's work on the Brain. That letter alone might be sufficient, if it

[1] Letter to Dr Tafel, April 21, 1882.
[2] Letter to Dr Tafel, July 8, 1882.
[3] Letter to Dr Tafel, July 20, 1882.

expressed any spiritual or moral horror of Vivisection. The work will lie under a ban unless that
is done, for the experiments recorded in it are
atrocious. And if Swedenborg arrived at his results
without such deeds, it would seem that he ought
not to be assumed as countenancing Vivisection
spiritually—which is what it will ultimately come
to—without some other reason being given for it
than his discoveries. If your work leads to the
supposition that he would join the Vivisectors now
that they are at the bar of Humanity, it will, I
believe, mislead the Youth of the New Church, who
are quite open to be misled ; as the recent discussion
in your Church shows.

"*I should not like to be mentioned in connexion
with the work unless the contrary position, on the
humane ground, is clearly pointed out.*"

Although he was keenly interested in all that
went on around him, to the end of his long life,
Wilkinson's active interests were too definitely
predisposed to allow him to drift into " a party
man " in politics. He had always certain questions
which he wished to have ventilated, certain wrongs
(always the wrongs of others) which he wished to
have righted. Wherever he scented oppression,
there he championed the oppressed, and was ready
to range himself aside those who were like-minded.
Early in his life, his keen sense of humour played
in genial irony upon those with whom he differed.

Later his unpopular predispositions brought about an isolation which he keenly felt but never bewailed ; and his method of attack was marked by stern but reasoned invective. This was nowhere more obvious than in the strong and public line which he took concerning the Contagious Diseases Prevention Acts of 1866 to 1869. These Acts provided for the compulsory examination of prostitutes in garrison towns by medical men, appointed for that purpose, and the segregation of those found dangerous to the community. This was regarded as state recognition of the evil which it was designed to check. Such measures had been common on the Continent, but their adoption in England was new, and it led to long and loud objection from many people and on many grounds. Wilkinson saw in it an outrage on womanhood at the instance of the medical profession who, through the Royal Colleges of Physicians and Surgeons, had memorialized Government in favour of extension of the areas to be affected, in 1869. He was soon characteristically busy, both publicly and privately, alone and in conjunction with others, in efforts to bring about the repeal of the laws in question.

In 1870 he issued a pamphlet on " The forcible Introspection of Women for the Army and Navy, considered physically," of which some mention has been made in the first chapter. In it he spared no effort to inspire pity for those whom he regarded as oppressed, and disgust against those whom he saw as their oppressors. It is unnecessary to quote what was intentionally painful in its effect upon the reader.

This pamphlet and another entitled " A Free State and Free Medicine " were Wilkinson's contributions to the agitation for the repeal of the Contagious Diseases Acts. They were highly approved by the associations working to that end, as the following letter from Mrs Josephine Butler, one of the prime movers therein, will show :—

[1] " I have read with great pleasure your tract, " A Free State and Free Medicine," and thank you with all my heart for your words. I wish we could have the pages relating to the C.D. Acts reprinted alone for our present purpose : they are so forcible.

" Yes, you say truly, *our* reasons for opposing the Acts are reasons of fire which will burn up any House of Commons which has not its legislation founded on a rock.

" I see the movement is beginning which I have long anticipated among the women of France. I should like to go over and help them—to build barricades, if need be, and to roast alive in the Tuilerie Gardens the Inspectors of Women, with their implements, as the Women of the Great Revolution roasted Lafayette's horse ! . . .

" I wish I could tell you what I have lately seen

[1] Letter from Mrs Josephine Butler, April 24, ? 1871.

and heard in Kent. I want to tell some good doctor what the women tell me of their *bodily* sufferings."

An old friend and patient, Francis W. Newman, the brother of the Cardinal, also wrote, in the following terms :—

[1] " Your pamphlet on ' Introspection, etc.,' reached me as I was starting for Manchester, to take part in meetings against this very matter and against Compulsory Vaccination. I read it in the train. On my return home, after staying with friends in two places, I found on my table your liberal parcel of twenty-five copies of the same pamphlet. My problem now is, how to distribute them judiciously. . . . But my immediate business is to express my thanks and my sense of the value of your brave contribution to truth, justice and mercy. As a man full grown in mind, you fearlessly assume your own style, which is neither mine nor that of any other man, but strictly yours ; and, as such, will give material for irrelevant attack to those who wince under the severity of your lash. But, in my full belief, you vindicate, by the weight and fulness of your matter, your right to assume your own manner : and when I get over the repulsiveness of the subject itself (doubly repulsive, when, with words so plain, you strip it of all disguise), I find in your treatment a lyrical and prophetic grandeur. Omitting here and there words which are not really

[1] Letter from Mr F. W. Newman, July 3, 1870.

needed, I have read out long portions to ladies, and find that they are felt to be beautiful as well as noble and valuable. *My* taste does require omissions of words which, nevertheless, may the better stab the dull senses of medical men stupefied by materialism. . . . I find it hard to estimate conjecturally whether your style will more entice or repel : for I think that different men will be differently affected. But in my own name I heartily thank you for fulfilling a painful task with vigour and faithfulness so unshrinking, and with a spirit of holiness which I hope will be diffusive. . . . I read two passages of your pamphlet to the Manchester meeting against the C.D. Acts."

It will be remembered that the question of the repeal of these acts was fiercely agitated and as fiercely opposed. A Royal Commission was appointed in 1871 ; a Special Commission was appointed in 1879. Though the majority of both reported in favour of a continuance of the Acts, a majority of the House of Commons condemned the principles of them in 1883, and the Acts themselves were repealed in 1886.

There are few things less profitable than tracing movements through old controversies. The bitterness and misunderstanding on both sides are painfully apparent. As the footsteps crush the old ashes, the dust of such things is ungrateful and distressing ; the generous heat which once brought them about has died away with the brains and hearts which evoked it. The student is tempted to think that the world would have been none the worse had neither fire nor ashes ever been. But it is in such struggles that character is educated and displayed; and to have faced unpopularity and disapproval for the sake of right, to have carried opposition on questions of principle through the evil days to success, is a discipline which strengthens and ennobles the man who has experienced it.

Few will be found to share Wilkinson's judgment in all the controversies in which he engaged, but still fewer will fail to see in him a clean and a hard fighter, ever actuated by fear of wrong and love of right. To those who saw him most clearly he was revealed as most loving and universally bene- volent. His attacks upon what he thought evil were tremendous and unsparing; his spirit of humble brotherhood to erring humanity was an essential part of his practical religion.

CHAPTER IV

APPRECIATIONS

THIS chapter is devoted to estimations of Garth Wilkinson's character and work from divers pens. It contains, however, no letters addressed to himself. When Boswell "presumed to animadvert" on Johnson's eulogy of Garrick in the "Lives of the Poets," Samuel defended himself by saying, "Why, sir, some exaggeration must be allowed"; and, by a parity of postulation, it is scarcely fair to expose the words of one who acknowledges a presentation copy to cold print after the lapse of years.

Robert Matheson, who himself wrote books too little known, under the pseudonym of "Corvichen," engaged for years in an intimate and candid correspondence with Garth Wilkinson. He wrote, on hearing of his friend's death :—[1]

" I had been thinking, some days before I received your note, of the Grand Old Man, and a vague feeling arose in me that he was away. Then I naturally thought of his wonderful vigour and his other great qualities—hardly a man like him anywhere. And

[1] Letter to Miss Florence Pertz, December 1, 1899.

so here is yet another Book published three days before his death !

" I have often tried to understand him, but always felt myself foiled in the attempt ; but one thing was and remains clear—that he was a prophet, or National Teacher, by character and calling. Two very necessary characteristics of a prophet seemed strong in him—heroic indignation and tenderness.

" No doubt he was widely known ; but it is astonishing how comparatively few know about him. The worse for them ! Prophets are not *popular* characters."

An old medical friend, upon the same occasion, wrote as follows :—

" I had the greatest possible admiration for Dr Wilkinson. I used often to say that I considered him, Dr Martineau and Ruskin the greatest masters of lucid, epigrammatic, terse, felicitous style in writing English, then living ; and that to those three I owed whatever facility in English composition I possessed. He altered his style of writing very much in his later publications, and, as I told him, I missed the felicity, the wit and fantasy of the older style. He wrote, during his last days, under a deeper sense of obligation to the truths which he felt himself commissioned to declare— and with less consciousness of his readers who could be either stirred or amused or excited by the force of his picturesque utterance. My knowledge of him dates from about the year 1851 or 2, when he became the medical attendant of my father and sister. I had known him by repute before that, as a friend also of my uncle, Dr Morell, and as a translator of Swedenborg. After that, I used often to see him, and always felt instructed and inspired by his conversation.

"I remember calling on him soon after he published his little volume of inspirational poems, and he told me how he produced them—putting his hand to paper and accepting any suggestion that rose in his mind. 'I will see what comes to my hand about you,' he said ; and as soon as his hand rested on the paper, he said : 'The first words are *he stands*,' and then the two following verses followed :—

> He stands upon a hill of green,
> Where flowers are rare and sad ;
> But brighter things are near him seen
> And things to make him glad.
>
> The sky hath openings when the earth
> Hath closed her to some (?) drear:
> Then gird thyself for spirit birth,
> And choke the snakes of fear.

"These verses accurately reflected the rather sad and sombre tinge of my mood and experiences at that time.

"I think your grandfather was a little disappointed

in me because I did not sufficiently enter into all his theological and philosophical teachings. In fact, I found it rather difficult to do so : as he grew older, if his thoughts grew deeper and more solemn, they also became to me less distinct. I could not follow their track at all times : and, when I did, I often felt dissent. . . . In fact I thought that the dear and venerable old Doctor was just a little intolerant, and standing aloof from some of the best tendencies of the time. But he was one of the grandest men I ever knew, and I shall always look back upon my friendship with him with pride and delight. I do not think Emerson's well-known eulogy was at all exaggerated."

In Volume III. of a New Series of *The University Magazine* there appeared a course of " Contemporary Portraits " of the eighteenth, of which Wilkinson was the subject. This " portrait," which was unsigned, appeared in the number for June 1879. As the most thorough examination of Wilkinson's work with which we are acquainted, extracts from it will be interesting, but it must be borne in mind that the estimation appeared full twenty years before that work was completed.

" Some there are who have burning things to say, and, avoiding the pitfalls that attend upon controversy, content themselves with saying their say, and, instead of bringing it by strenuous dissemination before the general public, bequeath it to such as may be sympathisers, and leave it to make its way abroad in due time through its own force and vehemence. They are glad to do without the sweets and sufferings, the perils and powers of modern notoriety, and to follow in the road of the philosophers of old time, who spoke only to such as had ears.

"The subject of the present sketch is known in one way or other to most of the bearers of the best-known names amongst us. In Mudie's Library there are probably next to no copies of any of his works; we do not remember to have seen him reviewed in either the *Daily Telegraph* or the *Saturday Review*; his books seem never to be advertised in the usual channels; but if such as Carlyle, Browning, Tennyson, Emerson, Longfellow, Hawthorne, were to be asked dubiously about him by someone who should think him obscure, one might perhaps have replied, ' I travelled with him ' ; another, ' He was a friend of my youth ' ; another, ' We have had long arguments together ' ; a fourth, ' I have taken his medicine ' ; a fifth, ' When I was once in great doubt, I drew much from him.'

"Without advertisement, our author's books find a public, and some to the extent of several editions. He has too broad and varied a field of work to be sectarian, but so far as he may go by that name, it is in connection with what is called the New Church, a body holding by the traditions as interpreted by Swedenborg. This little Church contains a large proportion of men who move in higher realms of thought than the members of most other sects, and no doubt the works of so large a thinker as Dr Wilkinson are especially esteemed among them. . . .

" At this early period of his life Dr Wilkinson showed that predilection for principles, whether as forming the basis of philosophy, or the guidance of physical research, which has shown itself so strongly in his later writings, and, coupled with the originality of his nature and force of his sympathies, has made him rather a religious political economist, than either a medical specialist or a Swedenborgian —long and ardently though he has dwelt upon the works of the Swedish seer. . . .

" The generality so prefer the trivial to the recondite that it is probable that the subjects upon which Dr Wilkinson has chosen to discourse have prevented his having due literary recognition as a master of English prose. The following, from his introduction to the 'Economy of the Animal Kingdom,' may serve as a specimen of his style.

" ' Accordingly he (Swedenborg) gives no bond to reconstruct society, nor professes to be able to drag the secrets of truth into day by an unerring or mechanical method; but having obtained a sufficiency of doctrinal implements for present use, and mindful that active life is the best lot of man

T

and the finest means of improvement, he builds such an edifice as his materials and opportunities permit, and arrives at such an end as a good man may be satisfied with. The perfecting of instruments he knows must be successive, but that the use of them must not be postponed, and therefore he lays out his possessions to the best advantage, in the confidence that this is the truest way to benefit posterity.'

" The following passages from the same work will instance both philosophy and style :—

" ' Reason is as the hand of man, but imagination is the *palpus* or tenaculum of human nature. Reason beholds the same surfaces as imagination, only it does not stop with the surface, but penetrates to the form and mechanism underlying the colour and shape of the object, being in fact that power which acknowledges the intrinsic solidity of nature.

" 'Great confusion has undoubtedly been introduced by regarding body as the same with matter. For body is the necessary ultimatum of each plane of creation, and thus there is a spiritual body as well as a natural body, and by parity of fact, there is a spiritual world as well as a natural world : but matter is limited to the lowest plane, where alone it is identical with body. There is no matter in the spiritual world, but there is body notwithstanding, or an ultimate form, which is less living than the interior forms ; which is the solid in relation to the fluid, the fibre and the skin and the membrane relatively to the living blood in its natural degrees.

" 'It is wrong therefore to attempt to transcend the fact of embodiment; the hope is mistaken that would lead us to endeavour thus after pure spirituality. The way to the pure spiritual is the moral, and the moral delights to exhibit itself in actions, and body is the theatre of actions, and by consequence the mirror and continent of the spiritual. . . .'

" A large portion of Dr Wilkinson's later writings is devoted to special topics, and seems to arise out of a consciousness on his part that the public requires protection against specialism of all kinds, which is apt to become despotism. Society at large is prone to deride such chivalrous championship as chimerical, and to trust blindly in the virtues of a majority, and the practical unimpeachableness of things as they are. But Dr Wilkinson looks deeper and sees wickedness to the poor and oppression of the weak, in the unquestioned action of powerful legalized cliques. As poor humanity was once overridden by priesthood, he appears to think it is in danger of being subjected to an equal tyranny from the high-priests of medical orthodoxy. There no doubt is a tendency to make certain questions " strictly professional," and to shut out from general un-professional humanity any right of forming an opinion upon important matters in regard to which

professional opinion insists upon being implicitly
accepted as final. As a matter of principle, Dr
Wilkinson is right, and he and his followers ought
to be welcomed as the protectors of lazy and ignorant
humanity. The majority of us have been vaccinated
at an age when we were too young to rebel; we are
not of the class that is subjected to forcible introspection; nor do we belong to the ranks of animals
used for vivisection; we are consequently inclined
to leave such matters alone, as not affecting
ourselves :—

"Let the galled jade wince, *our* withers are
unwrung. In politics alone we admit a majority to
honour, and that perhaps only in proportion to its
size. In matters that have to do with our bodies, we
are wont to take refuge in blind faith, or equally blind
distrust, in what is prescribed for us. Dr Wilkinson
sees danger in such conventional acceptance, and
finds in the governmental medical *régime* under
which we live, the same principle in action as
Le Sage saw in *Dr Sangrado*, the Hippocrates of
Valladolid. . . .

"This subject (compulsory vaccination) has
aroused Dr Wilkinson to most unphilosophical
wrath. We are so accustomed nowadays to writings
from which feeling is eliminated, and which have
a cold, and, so to speak, heartless regard to facts,
that Dr Wilkinson must no doubt to many seem
over-impetuous and lost in his own indignation.

The intellect by itself, when applied to the great problems of the world, and finding them hard to solve, is apt to become callous, and, leaving them alone, to busy itself with what it imagines it knows with certainty. We ought to be grateful to Dr Wilkinson for refusing to ignore even minor questions, or to treat them in any but the largest public light. In his philosophy, human life is integral, and to be reverenced in all its details, not for the sake of the details, but for the sacredness of the whole. Certain evils and compromises, despotisms of professional trades-unions, and callousness of licensed power, which press most heavily upon the poor, the weak and the obscure members of society, excite his indignation, as being violations of humanity. If he should found a school, it will be of those who are practical because they are first spiritual; and it may be found that the most consistently, minutely and intensely practical will be those whose perceptions are made keen and sensitive by marking the workings of spiritual laws, whereby the degradations of daily life impress the more distinctly, and stimulate them to a more earnest passion of effort to find the remedy. But to the sensual and slothful, the superficial and the selfish, it will at all times be difficult to distinguish the heightened insight and loving passion from fanaticism."

In *The Letters of Dante Gabriel Rosetti*, edited by Dr George Birkbeck Hill (page 201), we have an

interesting glimpse of Garth Wilkinson. Rosetti
wrote to Mr Allingham [near the end of 1862].

" You will remember my troubling you once or
twice about that *Bogie* poem book of Wilkinson's.
I am wanting it now to mention in a passage on
Blake's poetry which I am writing for the *Life*
never quite completed.   Could you kindly let me
have the loan of yours as soon as you can."

A note adds :—

" ' That Bogie poem ' was *Improvisations from the
Spirit* by Dr J. Garth Wilkinson, the homœopathist
who was Miss Siddal's physician in 1854. Hawthorne,
whose children he attended in December 1857,
wrote of him :—' He is a homœopathist, and is known
in scientific and general literature ; at all events,
a sensible and enlightened man, with an un-English
freedom of mind on some points. For example,
he is a Swedenborgian and a believer in modern
Spiritualism. He showed me some drawings that
had been made under the spiritual influence by a
miniature painter who possesses no imaginative
power of his own, and is merely a good mechanical
and liberal copyist ; but these drawings, representing angels and allegorical people were done by an
influence which directed the artistic hand, he not
knowing what his next touch would be, nor what
the final result.' . . . According to W. B. Scott,
' Emerson said, " Wilkinson was most like Bacon of
all men living." '   Scott adds that ' Wilkinson was

as tall and as straight as a spear, and looked steadily at you from behind his spectacles as if he saw your thoughts as distinctly as your nose, while Tennyson cared little and noted little of either.' "

We conclude our account of Garth Wilkinson with three extracts from obituary notices which closely followed his death.

From the *New Church Magazine*, November 1879.

" He was one of the most useful and ardent members of the Swedenborg Society. In the Society's rooms there is both a bust and a portrait of him. Kindly and genial, he won the affections of others. Keen in perception, he possessed a fluency enjoyed by very few. His later literary style was, in the opinion of some, a little too classic and ornate for modern taste, but none can doubt the vigour of his writing or the brilliancy of his illustrative power.

" Students of the human body not unfre-quently become materialists or agnostics. With Dr Wilkinson the perception of spiritual realities was as a fire to his bones. His 'Human Body and its Connection with Man' is one of the most vigorous pleas we know for the recognition of the spiritual nature of man.

" When we remember that his literary work was done in the leisure left from the active and onerous duties of his profession, it is clear that he must have been surpassingly industrious. . . .

" His influence has been widely felt; not only in the New Church but throughout the literary and philosophical world. An able physician, a clear thinker, an original and exceedingly industrious writer, he had won the respect and affection of all who knew him, and of many more who had not been privileged to enjoy personal intercourse with him. It would be wrong for us to grieve over-much, for we know that his profound convictions about the spiritual life are now being verified by him, and he will have the reward of the good works that follow a life industrious, full of zeal for the truth and earnest, self-sacrificing labour for the spiritual advancement of the world.   EDITOR."

From the *New Church Review*, January 1900.

In a review of " Isis and Osiris," under the title of " Dr Wilkinson's Last Book."

"   .   .   . In his dedicatory letter to Professor Wiedemann, of the University of Bonn, our author affirms, ' I have been inclined to give my book the additional name of a Tract for the Times '—a tract, we may suppose, for ' these vivisecting heathen times ' to borrow a very Wilkinsonian phrase found on one of the last pages in the volume.   And surely it is a noble and timely appeal to the present genera-tion, with dead ritual within the Church, and dead materialism both within and without, to open the lungs of intelligence to the Breath of the Lord of

Life. What we stand in need of to-day is a quickened sense of the Lord's presence as the life of this Universe and the soul of His Church. Dr Wilkinson's farewell word comes as an inspiration to a higher faith and larger trust. And now, having finished his work on earth, it is pleasant to think of his great and magnanimous soul in the fuller atmosphere of heavenly planes, where the Book of Respirations is open as the Book of the Lord's Life, and all the inhabitants are living breaths, animate with a divine influx.

" Coming of an old Durham family, Dr Wilkinson had many of the rugged North of England qualities, among them the gift of laconic and vigorous speech. He has often reminded his readers of Carlyle, and Emerson likened his rhetoric to ' the armoury of the invincible knights of old.' It is not easy, however, for everyone to read him. Many years ago, when ' The Human Body and its Connection with Man ' was published, Professor Bush praised the substance, but criticized what seemed to him the difficult and affected style. As a matter of fact, the book grew out of conversations which the author had with the late Henry James, who was then living in London, not far from the Doctor's office. A physician's life is exacting, and does not favour long periods of quiet composition and revision. The author of ' The Human Body ' and its numerous successors, thought out between times the manifold

points that commanded him and jotted them down
at odd moments of leisure. This professional handi-
cap, limiting his time of utterance, no doubt is largely
responsible for the oracular character of many of
his statements. Dr Wilkinson was simply surcharged
with the thought that was in him. Mr James
complained that Emerson's private thought and
conversation were incomparably inferior to his
public utterances. Dr Wilkinson exhibited most
markedly the opposite trait. His personality was
inspiring, and his private utterances on high themes
were crammed with vital meaning, and wore a
drapery of language that no polish of revision could
make more fit or graceful. To those who have
enjoyed this conversation, his books seem like the
recurrence of personal visits.

"The reader will get most from Dr Wilkinson's
writings by reading them leisurely, and taking
their thoughts as hints. The ideas are given as
suggestions, and stimulate the reader to individual
mental activity. There is a unity through all
these notes and comments, dealing with apparently
scattered topics, but the unity is not of literary
form and consistency, but of honest devotion to
truth and unimpeachable perception of spiritual
and divine verities.

"As a secular and lay student of spiritual things,
Dr Wilkinson's work is of unique value to the church.
He had no cheap antipathies to 'ecclesiasticism,'

although he kept aloof from organizations. He pursued his studies and lived his life as a private English gentleman, with broad sympathies with his time and wide knowledge of the international world. Most of our New Church writers become accustomed to accommodating themselves to the state of mind of those who are supposed to know comparatively little of spiritual truth. Hence we rarely have the expression of thought that is the full measure of the mind. Our writers and speakers are tethered by their avocation. Dr Wilkinson writes neither professionally nor professorially. His mind strikes out to utter itself, and not to come down to primary school demonstration. His books are the true expressions of the best reaches of his own mind. Hence the deepest student finds them virile and fecund. There is intellectual exhilaration in understanding them, and their originality and vitality make it impossible to skip them."

A notice of Garth Wilkinson's death appeared in the *Daily News*. Our extract betrays the practised and sympathetic hand of a dearly esteemed friend.

" Emerson's description of him as a ' startling re-appearance of Swedenborg after a hundred years ' had a certain literal significance. His mind was of exactly the same cast. It naturally and without effort, saw in every external fact only an inner spiritual significance. Phenomena, in their merely physical relations, seemed absolutely meaningless to him, and he moved amid ideas with a certainty that might have been envied by the most convinced materialist in his grasp of the ordinary facts of life. He was one of those born to believe. Personally he was a man of the sweetest and most winning nature and the gentlest disposition. He had survived nearly all his most eminent contemporaries, and, but for the care with which he was tended to the last by his own family, there would have been something of pathos in the solitude of his old age.''

INDEX

Trieste

Trieste Publishing has a massive catalogue of classic book titles. Our aim is to provide readers with the highest quality reproductions of fiction and non-fiction literature that has stood the test of time. The many thousands of books in our collection have been sourced from libraries and private collections around the world.

The titles that Trieste Publishing has chosen to be part of the collection have been scanned to simulate the original. Our readers see the books the same way that their first readers did decades or a hundred or more years ago. Books from that period are often spoiled by imperfections that did not exist in the original. Imperfections could be in the form of blurred text, photographs, or missing pages. It is highly unlikely that this would occur with one of our books. Our extensive quality control ensures that the readers of Trieste Publishing's books will be delighted with their purchase. Our staff has thoroughly reviewed every page of all the books in the collection, repairing, or if necessary, rejecting titles that are not of the highest quality. This process ensures that the reader of one of Trieste Publishing's titles receives a volume that faithfully reproduces the original, and to the maximum degree possible, gives them the experience of owning the original work.

We pride ourselves on not only creating a pathway to an extensive reservoir of books of the finest quality, but also providing value to every one of our readers. Generally, Trieste books are purchased singly - on demand, however they may also be purchased in bulk. Readers interested in bulk purchases are invited to contact us directly to enquire about our tailored bulk rates. Email: customerservice@triestepublishing.com

You May Also Like

Hour by Hour; Or, The Christian's Daily Life

E. A. L.

ISBN: 9780649607242
Paperback: 172 pages
Dimensions: 6.14 x 0.37 x 9.21 inches
Language: eng

Heath's Modern Language Series. Atala

François-René de Chateaubriand & Oscar Kuhns

ISBN: 9780649066155
Paperback: 144 pages
Dimensions: 6.14 x 0.31 x 9.21 inches
Language: eng

www.triestepublishing.com

You May Also Like

ISBN: 9780649724185
Paperback: 130 pages
Dimensions: 6.14 x 0.28 x 9.21 inches
Language: eng

Report of the Second Annual Meeting of the Maryland State Bar Association, Held at Ocean City, Maryland, July 28-29, 1897

Conway W. Sams

ISBN: 9780649640430
Paperback: 332 pages
Dimensions: 6.14 x 0.69 x 9.21 inches
Language: eng

The Works of James Russell Lowell, Vol. VII. The Poetical Works of James Russell Lowell, in Four Volumes, Vol. I

James Russell Lowell

You May Also Like

1807-1907 The One Hundredth Anniversary of the incorporation of the Town of Arlington Massachusetts

Various

Various

ISBN: 9780649420544
Paperback: 108 pages
Dimensions: 6.14 x 0.22 x 9.21 inches
Language: eng

Biennial report of the Board of State Harbor Commissioners, for the two fiscal years commencing July 1, 1890, and ending June 30, 1892

Various

Various

ISBN: 9780649194292
Paperback: 44 pages
Dimensions: 6.14 x 0.09 x 9.21 inches
Language: eng

www.triestepublishing.com

You May Also Like

ISBN: 9780649199693
Paperback: 48 pages
Dimensions: 6.14 x 0.10 x 9.21 inches
Language: eng

Biennial report of the Board of State Harbor Commissioners for the two fisca years. Commeneing July 1, 1884, and Ending June 30, 1886

Various

ISBN: 9780649196395
Paperback: 44 pages
Dimensions: 6.14 x 0.09 x 9.21 inches
Language: eng

Biennial report of the Board of state commissioners, for the two fiscal years, commencing July 1, 1890, and ending June 30, 1892

Various

Find more of our titles on our website. We have a selection of thousands of titles that will interest you. Please visit

www.triestepublishing.com

Lightning Source UK Ltd.
Milton Keynes UK
UKOW06f0849231017

311488UK00004B/552/P